ANTHONY BAKER

A Battlefield Atlas of the English Civil War

PRC

Key to Symbols on maps

BLACK is used to show Royalist regiments, commanders, etc, BLUE is used to show Parliamentarian equivalents.

 Regiments of foot*

 Regiments of horse*
*These are sometimes symbolic rather than the actual number of regiments.

 Dragoons

 Routes of march. Two commanders may be shown marching on the same route, although not necessarily at the same time. Straight lines are symbolic routes.

 Hills or higher ground

 Towns under siege. These are ringed in the colour of the besieging army.

 Roads

===== Tracks

RIVER···· Rivers

Coastlines

First published 1986 by Ian Allan Ltd

© Anthony Baker 1986

This edition published by
The Promotional Reprint Company Ltd
Kiln House, 210 New Kings Road,
London SW6 4NZ
exclusively for Bookmart Ltd
Desford Road, Enderby,
Leicester LE9 5AD

ISBN 1 85648 334 7

Printed and bound in China

Preface

MANY books have been written on a variety of aspects of the English Civil War — political, constitutional, the battles, arms, dress, organisation and so on. Most of them are scholarly, long and very detailed, and intended for readers who require such knowledge. On the other hand most books used in schools are lacking in detail, and in any case refer only to the main battles of Edgehill, Newbury, Marston Moor, Naseby, Dunbar and Worcester, the minor battles and campaigns being largely ignored.

This book is intended to bridge the gap and to present a comprehensive picture of the war, covering all the battles, actions and engagements in enough detail to make the background to the battles and their affect on the war understandable. It is hoped that it will paint a picture and tell the story of a very troubled period of English history, dominated by two implacable idealists, King Charles I and Oliver Cromwell, neither of whom (nor the people they governed), gained anything worthwhile from the disastrous events which they generated. If any good came from it at all, it was the realisation of the need for a Standing Army for Great Britain, which subsequently laid the foundations of a great Empire and the wealth gained by the country as a whole from the worldwide trade which it engendered.

For those readers who want more detail than this book can give within its limited format, three books are recommended. They are *The English Civil War* (1974) by Brigadier Peter Young, *The English Civil War* (1972) by John Tucker and Lewis S. Winstock, which gives an excellent account of the arms, weapons, dress and the organisation of the armies, and *Leaders of the Civil War* (1977) by Geoffrey Ridsdill Smith and Margaret Toynbee, which gives very detailed biographies of all the main characters involved.

Anthony Baker
Wendover, 1986

King Charles I (1600-1649)

Charles was born in 1600, the second son of James I, and became heir apparent on the death of his brother in 1612. He first wooed the Spanish Infanta, but failing there married the sister of Louis XIII of France, Henrietta Maria. He based all his constitutional and ecclesiastical policies on his belief in the Divine Right of Kings, that he was answerable to nobody but God for his actions. He battled ceaselessly with Parliament, but sealed his fate when he gave assent to the parliamentary Act of Attainder against the Earl of Strafford, after which Parliament gradually deprived him of all his royal and arbitrary powers. After the war he might have saved his life and kingdom by compromising with the Presbyterian Scots, but that he would not do. He was tried for treason before an unconstitutional and illegal tribunal and condemned to death, being beheaded in Whitehall on 29 January 1649, and subsequently was regarded as a martyr.

All photographs courtesy National Portrait Gallery, unless otherwise indicated

MAP 1

Battlefields and Main Towns of the English Civil War

Causes and Background

THE English Civil War was actually three separate wars, covering the periods 1642-46, 1647-48 and 1650-51, each representing a distinct phase of the overall conflict. It was a traumatic period for the people of these islands. There had been other civil wars, but the most recent, the Wars of the Roses, had been almost 200 years before, and they had always been fought between limited constitutional or religious factions and had not involved the people as a whole.

The causes this time, in broadest terms, were a mixture of the religious, constitutional and economic, each affected by the situation in Europe. Loyalties were mainly geographical although other special factors had their effect. The poorer and pastoral shires, for example the north, northwest, southwest and Wales, were mostly Royalist, whereas the more prosperous counties in the south and London, where the monied merchants were numerous, supported Parliament. Even so the loyalties of areas and persons changed during the war, sometimes more than once.

It was in no sense a class war because families of all strata of society were frequently split between one side or the other. Father fought against son, brother against brother, and even some of Oliver Cromwell's relatives fought as Royalists. The first Roundhead army contained a number of peers, and this to a large extent continued throughout the war, and nearly half the Commons supported the King.

But to get even an outline of the causes of this sad affair one must go back 40 years to the ascent of James 1, sometimes and for good reason called the 'wisest fool in Christendom'.

On his accession in 1603 the English Puritans hoped that, with his Scottish Presbyterian upbringing, James would support them and their efforts towards Church reform, in particular the removal of the episcopacy; but they were to be sadly mistaken. Parliament, consisting exclusively of the propertied classes, maintained that it owed its privilege to

right and not to the King's Grace, but it too was to be disillusioned. And these two rejections turned Parliament against the King.

The disagreements were accentuated by lack of money. James had inherited a substantial deficit from Queen Elizabeth and efforts to reduce this, coupled with the influx of precious metals from the New World and the almost more precious spices from the Far East, created high inflation.

To make matters worse James was personally extravagant, lavishing money on his favourites in spite of the efforts of his chief adviser Robert Cecil, Earl of Salisbury, to reduce expenditure by removing their pensions and sinecures. Some money was obtained from the traditional feudal dues and customs duties, an increase in which upset both the aristocratic and monied classes. Parliament refused to grant him any more money, and in fact tried to ban the feudal dues which would only have made the matter worse; all his schemes for raising money seemed to create objections in one section of Parliament or another.

But money he had to have, and to that end he sold Crown lands, which denied him the rents and the obedience of his erstwhile tenants, and sold titles of nobility, which devalued the prestige of the Lords by introducing a commercial, as opposed to a landowning, aristocracy. When all else failed James levied taxes by Royal Prerogative, further alienating Parliament which now accused him of tactless and wanton use of his power. Gradually the King and his Ministers had lost control of Parliament.

Charles I came to the throne in 1625. He was a serious man, orderly and solemn but lacking in self-confidence and a sense of humour. He often had excellent ideas, but when his advisers did not agree with them (usually for selfish reasons) he was seldom confident enough to carry them out. Although Charles did not follow his father's pattern of keeping a Court of 'gaudy young men', he had his favourites, who were amassing power and money. The Court in which he lived was aloof from the people, and he lived extravagantly which alienated those paying taxes for its upkeep; he did not understand the common man and was unable to judge the feelings of his people and to realise the strength of their animosity, since his courtiers, for their own benefit, made sure that no information could reach him which might have allowed him to do so.

These fatal flaws in his character, and the lack of money, finally brought ruin to his regime, and his execution. Even so, the early opposition to the King did not anticipate or want his deposition but was intended only to rescue him from his Popish advisers and environment.

Charles inherited his father's financial problems and in particular one of the major causes of them, the Duke of Buckingham, whose cripplingly expensive foreign policies drove the country into wars with France and Spain. In a country strongly opposed to Catholicism, Buckingham arranged a marriage between Charles and the French princess Henrietta Maria and then promised to help Richelieu to subdue the Huguenots, who were Calvinists and therefore closely associated with the Puritans. Parliament showed its objection by withholding from the King the traditional life-time grant of Tunnage and Poundage, taxes on imports and exports. Charles therefore followed his father's example by levying them by Royal Prerogative and at the same time imposed a very unpopular capital levy.

In these adverse conditions Buckingham changed his policies and mounted a ruinously expensive and unsuccessful expedition to relieve the siege of the Huguenot stronghold at La Rochelle. This was not sufficient to satisfy his enemies and he was assassinated by the Puritan John Felton in 1628. Parliament now relented a little and granted the King the right to Tunnage and Poundage, but for one year only, which infuriated him because it appeared that Parliament was trying to control him. In 1629 Charles declared that princes were not bound to give account of their actions — claiming he had a Divine Right to rule — dissolved Parliament and proceeded to rule without it for the next 11 years.

Shortly after his dissolution of Parliament a religious conflict arose to further complicate matters. In 1633 William Laud, apparently having High Church leanings and having already been accused of Popery, was appointed Archbishop of Canterbury. In fact he was a moderate Protestant, but he was strongly opposed to Calvinism and saw this as a threat to the Establishment. The Puritans, on the other hand, saw Laud, backed by the King and his mistrusted Catholic wife, as a threat to their existence. The Puritans believed in predestination, that men could worship without the aid of clergy, that preaching was more important than prayer and that most ritual should be eliminated from church services.

Laud's insistence on the letter of the Law of the Church and on clergymen wearing surplices, and his rejection of the Puritan ideas of predestination, made him unpopular not only with the Puritans but with many other Protestants as well. Parliament supported the Puritans, but Laud's more outspoken opponents were dealt with severely, Prynne and others being publicly mutilated. This created uproar, not at the punishments themselves which were relatively commonplace, but because the recipients were gentlemen, normally safe from corporal punishment other than execution.

While this dissent was raging Charles made peace with Spain, minted bullion for payment of Spanish troops fighting the Protestants in Holland and allowed Spanish ships to use English ports en route to war. His support for Catholic France and his failure to support adequately the Protestant cause during the 30 Years War created further enemies. Little more would be needed to create a real explosion of popular feeling.

Still beset by money problems, Charles in 1634 again levied Ship Money. This was originally a requirement that coastal towns should provide ships for the Navy, or the money for them, and had later been extended to inland counties; but it had not been used as a tax for some years. In a sense the new levy was justifiable because there was now a real need for the navy to match the increasing strengths of the French and Spanish navies, but his opponents hotly contested the levy as it was seen as a means of providing money without recalling Parliament, which could not then exercise any constraint on him. Even Sir Ralph Hopton, a strong Royalist supporter in the west and later to become one of its chief generals, and Cornwall, later most Royalist of counties, opposed it.

In 1637 John Hampden, a wealthy Buckinghamshire landowner and a Member of Parliament, refused to pay Ship Money and was taken to court. Although the case went against him the verdict was close and was seen as a moral victory for Charles's enemies. The judgement was taken by many as an excuse not to pay the tax and the resulting confiscation of property in lieu raised a further storm.

Events now turned to Scotland, where James I had reintroduced bishops into Scotland, which was very unpopular. Charles demanded the return of ex-church lands from the nobles who had obtained them illegally and imposed the new liturgy — which was even more unpopular. The Scots therefore signed the Covenant which abolished episcopacy and re-established Presbyterianism, and then raised an army under Alexander Leslie, largely officered by men who had gained experience in Europe during the 30 Years War, to respond to Royal threats of action against them.

Charles with an untrained army, marched against the Scots. The expedition was a fiasco and he was forced to sign a treaty of surrender at Berwick, but he had not given up hope. He summoned Thomas Wentworth, Earl of Strafford, a man hated by the Puritans because, having been a supporter of Parliament in the 1620s, he had subsequently accepted a peerage and the Lord Lieutenancy of Ireland. On Strafford's advice Charles summoned Parliament and demanded money for a Scottish war. It refused to help unless its grievances on taxation were redressed, and although Charles agreed to abandon Ship Money (largely uncollectable in any case), it still refused to grant money and was rapidly dissolved. This was the Short Parliament.

In 1640 Charles set out on another invasion of Scotland without the money; Strafford fell ill, the troops deserted and mutinied because they were not being paid, and once more there was a fiasco with the rout of the army at Newburn near Newcastle. The Scots could now force a settlement, which allowed them to stay in Northumbria, but they also demanded indemnity and Charles was again forced to call Parliament. But now Parliament held the whip hand because Charles dared not dissolve it until he got his money: this again was refused. The affair resulted in what became known as the Long Parliament, which made its presence felt to Charles's discomfiture. Pym, its leader, exploited the situation to the full and Strafford and Laud were sent to the Tower. An Act of Attainder was passed and, despite Charles's personal attempt to rescue him, Strafford was executed in 1641, although Laud was to survive a little longer. Parliament now passed the Triennial Act which allowed it to meet at least once every three years without being summoned by the King, dissolved the Prerogative Courts including the Star Chamber, declared all taxes not sanctioned by Parliament (including Ship Money) illegal, and finally decreed that it could not be dissolved without its own consent. Charles was completely hog-tied.

Strafford's withdrawal from Ireland allowed power there to be gained by the Puritan Lords Justices. The Catholic Irish rebelled immediately and tried to oust the English and Scots from Ulster and elsewhere. Dublin castle was attacked unsuccessfully, but hundreds of Protestants were butchered and the atrocities were magnified in England. Parliament accused the Royalists of helping to raise the rebellion but could no nothing to suppress it without the use of a Royalist army, to which it would not consent. The situation was deteriorating rapidly.

Charles was still confident of ultimate support from the people and even from Parliament, and made promises of constitutional reform, but Pym and the Puritans in Parliament did not trust the King to honour them. Charles took advantage of agitation in London and attempts to prevent the bishops from taking their seats in the Lords, and of a rumour that the Commons intended to impeach the Queen, and ordered the impeachment of his extreme Parliamentary antagonists — Pym, Hampden, Hesilrige, Holles, Strode and Lord Mandeville (the future Earl of Manchester and Parliamentary commander) — hoping thereby that Parliament could exert a more conservative and sympathetic control.

On 4 January the King appeared personally at the Commons, with a large band of armed followers, to arrest the five Members; this was another major tactical error because they had disappeared after a 'leak' of his intentions by one of the Queen's Ladies in Waiting. When on the following day he ordered an attack on the City to arrest the Members, the gates were closed against him. Charles left London five days later and set up his Court at Hampton Court. He never returned to London except as a captive.

Again the King accepted bad advice, this time from the Queen and her supporters, to quell the rebellion with force. He sent the Queen abroad to raise money and troops, if necessary by selling the Crown Jewels, and marched to York, which he entered on 19 March 1642. Many Members of Parliament, seeing war approaching and alarmed by the radical actions of Parliament itself and the mob violence which was growing in London and elsewhere, left London to join Charles in York. Parliament, now almost totally Puritan, passed the Militia Bill giving authority to the Lords Lieutenants of the counties to raise troops on its behalf. But Parliament, in its euphoria, also now made a mistake by proposing a Bill which would have given it sovereignty and which threatened Parliamentary despotism, and this extremism helped to rally support to the King. On 12 June Charles issued Commissions of Array embodying county militias for his support. In July Parliament voted to raise an army under the Earl of Essex to fight the King.

The navy, small but with well trained and competent officers and crews, had been badly treated by the King and declared almost unanimously for Parliament. This gave Parliament a great advantage as the navy could protect communications with Continental friends and blockade Royalist supplies, and also had the effect of deterring foreign help for the King. Also, the only quick way of moving troops and armaments around the country was by sea, and most ports were held for Parliament.

There was no standing army, although there were small garrisons in the coastal fortresses: the armies for the war were raised from scratch, as had always been done for foreign expeditions. There were some experienced soldiers available, but most of the recruits were the unemployed and the sweepings of the country. The Trained Bands and the militia existed in each county for defence only and were largely untrained; only those in London, where there were eight regiments, were properly trained. There were also military societies in London which had been maintained by enthusiasts, two in particular being the Artillery Garden (which still exists as the Honourable Artillery Company) and the Military Garden, and these provided officers for the Trained Bands and later for the Parliamentary armies. But the Trained Bands would not fight far outside their home territories, as both armies were to discover.

Thus the standard of the armies which were to fight the English Civil War was, certainly at the start, very poor. They often deserted or muntinied, partly through lack of payment and partly because the armies had been raised with very little knowledge of the allegiances of different parts of the country. But with all the problems the scene was now set for one of the most damaging periods in the history of England.

It is of interest to note that the terms Cavalier for the Royalists and Roundhead for the Parliamentarians had first been used as epithets of reproach and disapprobation during the rioting outside the Houses of Parliament in 1641. They are not used in most narratives until early in 1643, by which time they had become titles of honour.

When King Charles marched to York his primary objective was to capture Hull, where the arsenal had been stocked for the war against Scotland; the Earl of Northumberland, the Lord High Admiral, was ordered to carry out this task. However, the Earl pleaded ill health to avoid commitment, perhaps because he was uncertain of his allegiance, perhaps because he was being coerced by Parliament to appoint his deputy, the Earl of Warwick, to carry out the same task on its behalf! The King then appointed Sir John Pennington as commander of the navy in the north, but whilst the arguments continued, Parliament stole a march on the King by sending ships to Hull to secure the port.

On 29 April Charles reached Hull by land and was refused entry to the town by the Parliamentary governor, Sir John Hotham. The contents of the arsenal were quickly loaded on to the Parliamentary ships and sent to London, an early disaster for the King. After more delay the Earl of Lindsey invested the town on 10 July but was unable to capture the port. Shortly afterwards Sir John Meldrum arrived by sea with a small force and, after some desultory fighting and the bombardment of the forts, drove off the investing army.

Early in August Prince Rupert and Prince Maurice arrived in Tynemouth from Holland to join the King. Meanwhile Charles had left York and raised his Standard at Nottingham. The Royalist army consisted of eight regiments of horse, 15 regiments of infantry and one regiment of dragoons, from which can be seen the support from the landed gentry and their families, who normally joined their regiments with their own horses. The regiments had no specific establishments and they varied considerably in size, being largely conditioned by the power of the commanders to recruit them.

The Earl of Essex had been appointed Captain General of the Parliamentary army, but had delayed joining his troops because he had been disputing with Parliament the title of Lord High Constable, which would have enabled him to treat directly with the King. Parliament had refused this and he now joined his army at Northampton on 10 September, taking with him his coffin and his escutcheon in case he should need them at his funeral!

The Parliamentary army consisted of six regiments of horse, 20 regiments of foot — each when up to strength of about 400 and 1,200 men respectively — and some dragoons. Sir John Merrick was Major General, although he was replaced by Philip Skippon after the battle of Edgehill. The Lord General of Horse was the Earl of Bedford with Sir William Balfour as Lieutenant General, and the Train of Artillery was commanded by the Earl of Peterborough. The regiments of foot were commanded, sometimes only in name, by the Earl of Essex, Sir John Merrick, the Earl of Peterborough, the Earl of Stamford, Lord Say, Lord Wharton, Lord Rockford, Lord St John, Lord Brooke, Lord Mandeville, Lord Robartes, Sir William Constable, Sir William Fairfax, Sir John Meldrum and Colonels Cholmondely, Holles, Bamfield, Grantham, Ballard and Charles Essex. The regiments of horse were commanded by the Earl of Bedford, Lord Fielding, Lord Willoughby of Parham, Sir William Balfour, Sir William Waller and Colonel Sands.

The allotment of regiments to brigades on both sides was entirely ad hoc, largely depending on who was available and the disposition of forces, and in any case this only applied in major battles. Mobile forces were of indeterminate strength and depended on the manpower available, often being strengthened by recruits gathered en route. After major battles the recruitment of replacements was often very slow, particularly as the war dragged on.

Robert Devereux, Earl of Essex (1591-1648)

Essex was eldest son of Queen Elizabeth I's favourite, and served abroad as a young man. He joined the Parliamentary army in 1642 and was made Commander-in-Chief. He resigned after his defeat at Lostwithiel, dying in London just as the war ended.

MAP 2

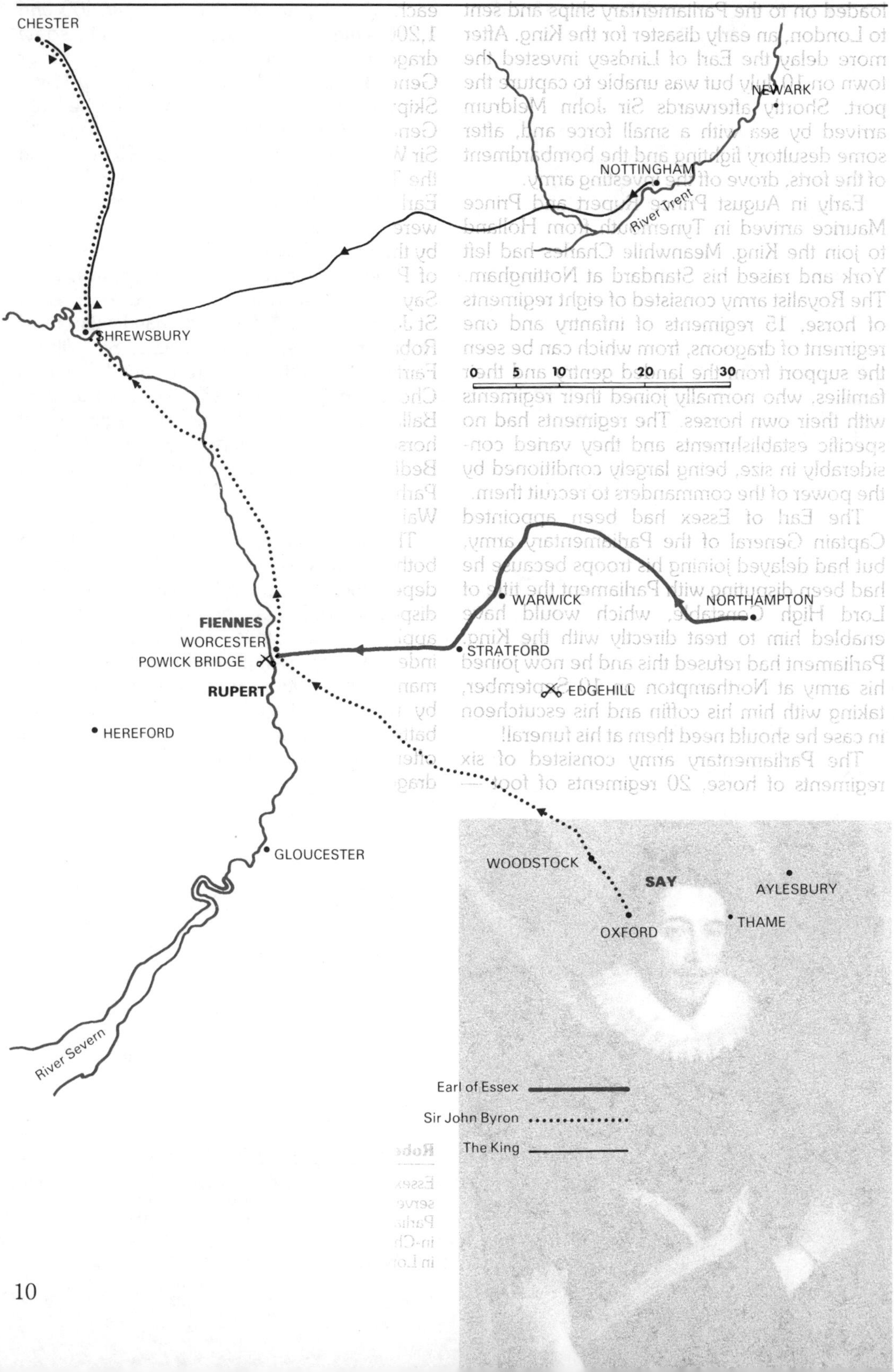

CHESTER

NEWARK

NOTTINGHAM

River Trent

SHREWSBURY

0 5 10 20 30

WARWICK

NORTHAMPTON

FIENNES

WORCESTER

STRATFORD

POWICK BRIDGE

RUPERT

EDGEHILL

HEREFORD

GLOUCESTER

River Severn

WOODSTOCK

SAY

AYLESBURY

OXFORD

THAME

Earl of Essex ━━━━━

Sir John Byron ∙∙∙∙∙∙∙∙∙∙∙∙∙

The King ━━━━━

The First Civil War

MAP 2

Powick Bridge and other Minor Actions

13-23 September 1642

ESSEX intended to march upon the King at Nottingham, but Charles, in spite of recruits coming in from Yorkshire, Staffordshire and Lincolnshire, was not yet strong enough to give battle. He disarmed the local Trained Bands which were hostile to him and set off for Chester, hoping to gain more support from Ireland and Wales. He occupied Shrewsbury on 20 September and Chester three days later. As at Nottingham the local gentry flocked to him, and he gained some new recruits from Wales, but many of the townspeople supported the Puritans and overall he got less support than he had hoped.

A Parliamentary force under Lord Say had occupied Oxford on 12 September. The Royalist commander, Sir John Byron, had left the city with as much University silver as he could collect and reached Worcester, where he was joined by Prince Rupert two days later. Essex also moved towards Worcester, via Coventry, Stratford and Warwick, and his troops were eager for battle. On 23 September Prince Rupert, realising that the city was indefensible, moved out southwards to cover Byron's departure to join Charles.

Near Powick Bridge Rupert met a body of about 1,000 Parliamentary horse under Nathaniel Fiennes and seizing the opportunity he quickly charged them. The fight took place in a narrow lane with no room for the Parliamentarians to manoeuvre, Rupert gained the advantage of the attacker against opposition which was somewhat lethargic and unwilling once it saw what war was all about, and the Parliamentary force broke and fled for miles. The skirmish did not save Worcester which was evacuated by Rupert the following day, and the fray was claimed by Parliament as a major victory. Even in those days propaganda based on falsehood was a powerful weapon!

Elsewhere in the country a number of local struggles were taking place. Part of Essex's army had occupied Hereford; the governor of Portsmouth, Lord George Goring, who had defected to the King after being appointed by Parliament, was forced to surrender by Sir William Waller, and was banished; the Marquess of Hertford, having been besieged in Sherborne Castle, now abandoned it and crossed into South Wales to organise resistance for the King there; Sir Ralph Hopton set off for Cornwall to raise support for the King, with little immediate success although shortly afterwards the county declared for Charles; the Royalist Earl of Derby gave up his siege of Manchester; and a younger member of the Hotham family captured Cawood castle for Parliament.

Both sides were still desperately short of money, but whereas the Parliamentary army could only gain this by increasing taxation, from which the Commons shrank as it knew that the London merchants would refuse, the King was able to supplement his treasury by the sale of peerages to the rich and from plate given to him by Royalist supporters to be melted down for coin, although this was still a drop in the ocean of his needs. The Queen's efforts to raise money and troops in Holland also met with little success — after all she was a Catholic begging in a strongly Lutheran country.

MAP 3

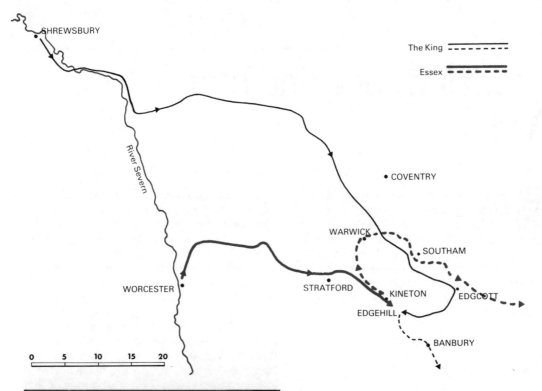

SHREWSBURY

The King ----------

Essex ==========

River Severn

• COVENTRY

WARWICK

SOUTHAM

WORCESTER •

STRATFORD

KINETON

EDGCOTT

EDGEHILL

BANBURY

0   5   10   15   20

Prince Rupert (1619-1682)

Nephew of the King and son of the 'Winter Queen', he
fought in the Thirty Years War and joined the Royalists in
1642. He was a brilliant soldier, revolutionised cavalry
tactics and was a good strategist, who might have saved
the Royalist cause if the King had taken his advice more
often. In 1644 he became Commander-in-Chief, but other
commanders and advisers were jealous of him. After the
Restoration he returned to England to the more peaceful
pursuits of art and science; it was he who founded the
Hudson Bay Company.

MAP 3

The Approaches to Edgehill

12-22 October 1642

ON 12 October Charles left Shrewsbury and set out for London, bypassing the Parliamentary strongholds of Warwick and Coventry, and the Earl of Essex marched on a parallel route to his west, although this proximity apparently did not bother either of them. On 21 October the King reached Southam, and Edgcott the following day, the way being clear for London. At Edgcott he heard that Essex was only seven miles away at Kineton, and Prince Rupert, realising the danger of moving on without fighting Essex, persuaded the King to occupy the brow of the ridge known as Edgehill. The first major battle of the Civil War was about to begin, 300 years to the day before the the start of the battle of Alamein.

Unlike Charles, Essex had no idea that the enemy was so close, but on the way to church (it being Sunday), he received the information and immediately deployed his army, although this took some time. Each army totalled about 14,000 men.

Essex drew up his troops some distance from the foot of the hill and the Royalists, as the attackers, had no option but to descend the slopes of Edgehill (then bare but now well wooded), and they formed a line roughly through Radway village. Charles's soldiers believed that victory must be theirs, as many thought that the enemy would refuse to fight against the King in person. However, Prince Rupert, although a brilliant soldier, had already in his few days in England antagonised

some of the Royalist army commanders; and as General of Horse he was exempted by the King from taking orders from the Earl of Lindsey, the Commander-in-Chief, who did not relish commanding an army in which he had no control of his cavalry. Lindsey complained to the King, but getting no satisfactory response resigned his command and his authority and returned to fight with his regiment. He was replaced by an experienced soldier, Patrick Ruthven, Earl of Forth, who was given little authority at all.

The layout of both armies on the ground was similar, with infantry in the centre, cavalry on each wing and dragoons covering the advances from the flanks. It is probable that each Royalist brigade deployed its foot regiments in a 'V' formation, the contemporary Swedish fashion, rather than in the straight lines of the Dutch.

The main body of Royalist horse was on the right under Rupert with a smaller force on the left under Lord Wilmot. Opposite Wilmot was Lord Fielding's regiment of horse, with those of Sir Philip Stapleton and Sir William Balfour in reserve, whilst opposite Rupert was Sir James Ramsay's horse, in which was included the troop of the unaptly named Sir Faithful Fortescue who did not support the Puritan cause and had promised to desert as soon as the battle was joined. The Royalists had five brigades of infantry in the centre, whilst the Parliamentarians had three brigades plus two independent regiments.

MAP 4

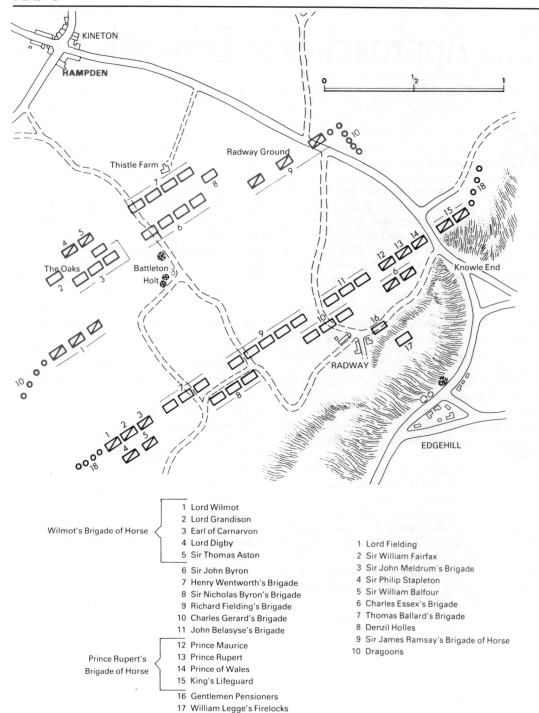

KINETON

HAMPDEN

0 ½ 1

Thistle Farm

Radway Ground

The Oaks

Battleton
Holt

Knowle End

RADWAY

EDGEHILL

Wilmot's Brigade of Horse
- 1 Lord Wilmot
- 2 Lord Grandison
- 3 Earl of Carnarvon
- 4 Lord Digby
- 5 Sir Thomas Aston

- 6 Sir John Byron
- 7 Henry Wentworth's Brigade
- 8 Sir Nicholas Byron's Brigade
- 9 Richard Fielding's Brigade
- 10 Charles Gerard's Brigade
- 11 John Belasyse's Brigade

Prince Rupert's
Brigade of Horse
- 12 Prince Maurice
- 13 Prince Rupert
- 14 Prince of Wales
- 15 King's Lifeguard

- 16 Gentlemen Pensioners
- 17 William Legge's Firelocks
- 18 Dragoons

- 1 Lord Fielding
- 2 Sir William Fairfax
- 3 Sir John Meldrum's Brigade
- 4 Sir Philip Stapleton
- 5 Sir William Balfour
- 6 Charles Essex's Brigade
- 7 Thomas Ballard's Brigade
- 8 Denzil Holles
- 9 Sir James Ramsay's Brigade of Horse
- 10 Dragoons

MAP 4

The Battle of Edgehill

23 October 1642

AFTER some desultory artillery fire at the beginning of the battle, in the early afternoon, Prince Rupert decided to charge the flank of the enemy cavalry. He was joined as promised by Fortescue, and put the whole of Ramsay's Parliamentary horse on that flank to flight, breaking up four infantry regiments in the confusion, although in some accounts it is said that these regiments had already run before the battle started. Rupert followed in hot pursuit, the horse now largely out of control, and took little part or interest in the battle from then on. He reached Kineton, which the troops plundered, and was only stopped eventually by two of Hampden's regiments coming up with the Puritan reserve. On the left Wilmot too charged and routed Fielding's regiment, also following in pursuit and joined against orders by Sir John Byron's regiment. Even the King's bodyguard galloped off after Rupert, and within minutes the Royalist army was left with no cavalry at all, which was a disaster because the regiments of Balfour and Stapleton remained unscathed. Nevertheless it seemed at this stage that the Parliamentary army might be completely destroyed.

The Royalist foot in the centre now joined the attack but met with stubborn resistance from the remaining Puritan regiments until it was charged and routed by Balfour and virtually ceased to exist. The Royalist foot on the right stood firm but took little active part in the early conflict; the Royal Foot Guards also stood and bore the brunt of the attacks against them for the rest of the day. But the odds were against them and eventually pressure from two regiments of foot and from Balfour's and Stapleton's horse broke them: the combat became fiercer and the casualties high.

Sir Edmund Verney, the Royal Standard Bearer, was killed by a member of Essex's Lifeguard (which after the Restoration became part of the present Life Guards) and the Standard was snatched from his dying hand. Lord Lindsey was mortally wounded and captured, and many other well known Royalists were killed. The remaining Parliamentary regiments were about to attack to finish off the Royalist army when they were assailed in the nick of time by the return of Rupert's cavalry, and withdrew from the field. Night was falling and both sides were exhausted, so the armies disengaged and camped where they were on the battlefield. The Royalists returned up Edgehill the following morning.

One fascinating detail needs chronicling. It is said — although there are other versions of the affair — that Captain John Smith of the King's Lifeguard, learning of the loss of the Royal Standard, picked up an orange scarf as worn by the Parliamentarians for identification, and with this disguise went into the enemy ranks with a couple of friends. He found the Standard in the hands of Essex's secretary and, telling him that such a prize could not remain in the hands of a common penman, took it from him, escaping from the enemy lines in the darkness. He returned the Standard to the King and was knighted on the spot.

MAP 5

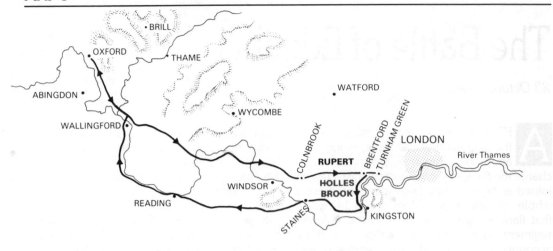

BRILL

OXFORD

THAME

WATFORD

ABINGDON

WYCOMBE

WALLINGFORD

COLNBROOK

TURNHAM GREEN

BRENTFORD

LONDON

RUPERT

River Thames

HOLLES BROOK

WINDSOR

READING

STAINES

KINGSTON

The King's March _____

```
0     5    10           20
```

Queen Henrietta Maria (1609-1669)

Henrietta Maria was the youngest daughter of King Henry IV of France and was born in Paris in 1609. She was betrothed to Charles when she was 15 and married to him by proxy after his accession in 1625. She was extravagant and very fond of gaiety, but antagonised many of the people by her partiality for the Roman Catholics. After raising much material for the war on the Continent, she left England in 1644 and never saw Charles again. She returned to England in 1660, but died at Colombes near Paris in 1669.

MAP 5

Brentford and Turnham Green

24 October 1642–January 1643

O N THE day following the Battle of Edgehill, Essex withdrew to Warwick, and both sides claimed the victory. The immediate fruits of victory undoubtedly lay with the King as his way was now clear to London, but he had not gained the strategic victory which he needed, and the probability of future success equally undoubtedly lay with Parliament since the Royalists had not been able to destroy them and had only just staved off defeat. Parliament now realised, to its surprise, that the King had a large and competent army, and the King learned from the heavy casualties his army had suffered just what the war would entail.

Charles marched on towards London, captured Banbury four days later, and on 29 October entered Oxford in triumph. From Oxford the King moved to Reading and then on to Colnbrook on 11 November, heading for London and bypassing Windsor, which had refused to surrender to Rupert.

Charles was, characteristically, being unduly cautious, not knowing exactly where Essex's army was. As a result Essex reached London first, which he should not have been able to do, and was able to organise its defences with his army and the 8,000-strong Trained Bands in the city. But before he could achieve this totally Prince Rupert attacked the outpost at Brentford on 12 November in heavy mist, overwhelmed the regiments of Denzil Holles and Lord Brooke which were defending the town, and sacked it.

By now the capital was aroused and troops poured out of London, and at Turnham Green Charles found his way barred by 24,000 men. Another 3,000 men under Sir James Ramsay were at Kingston, although this force was in the process of withdrawing to London Bridge to defend the southern approaches to the city. In the face of such opposition the King withdrew slowly to Kingston, where he was received with a warm welcome, then to Reading. He again reached Oxford, which became the Royalist headquarters for the remainder of the war, a fortnight later. It was the closest he ever got to London as a free man.

In Oxford, which became more of a garrison city than a university city, the King established his Court at Christchurch, while Rupert moved into St John's College where he had been entered as an undergraduate during a visit to England in 1636. A number of other colleges were used for various purposes. The Council met in Oriel, All Souls became an arsenal, and New College a magazine. The Astronomy and Music schools became tailors' shops where tailors laboured making uniforms for the Royalist troops, and New Inn Hall was turned into a mint.

As winter approached, major hostilities ceased but minor actions continued all over the country. In the south Lord Wilmot seized Marlborough on 5 December, and Charles established defensive garrisons around Oxford at Banbury, Brill, Abingdon, Wallingford, Faringdon and Burford. His strategic plan, now that his direct assault on London had been foiled, was to capture the rest of the country and surround London. But the Parliamentarians were already established in many areas and time would be needed to defeat them.

MAP 6

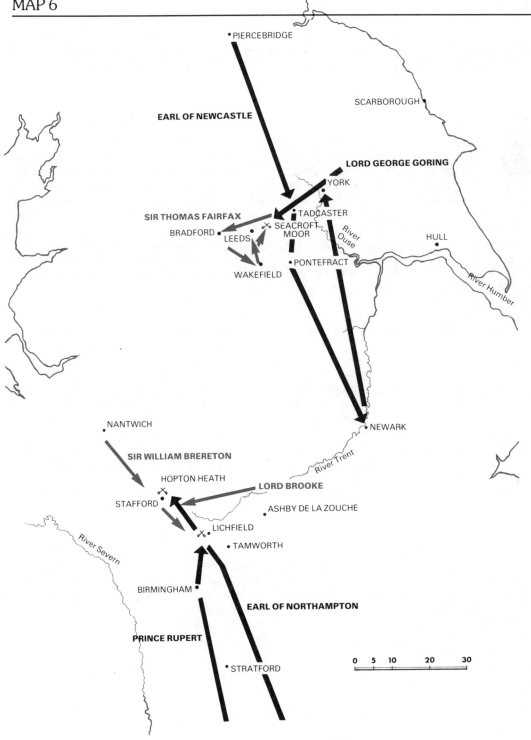

PIERCEBRIDGE

SCARBOROUGH

EARL OF NEWCASTLE

LORD GEORGE GORING

YORK

TADCASTER

SIR THOMAS FAIRFAX

BRADFORD

LEEDS

SEACROFT MOOR

River Ouse

HULL

PONTEFRACT

WAKEFIELD

River Humber

NANTWICH

NEWARK

SIR WILLIAM BRERETON

River Trent

HOPTON HEATH

LORD BROOKE

STAFFORD

ASHBY DE LA ZOUCHE

LICHFIELD

TAMWORTH

River Severn

BIRMINGHAM

EARL OF NORTHAMPTON

PRINCE RUPERT

STRATFORD

| 0 | 5 | 10 | 20 | 30 |

MAP 6

Hopton Heath, Seacroft Moor and Lichfield

5 December 1642–13 May 1643

LORD Newcastle, in command of all Royalist forces in the North, won an action against the younger Hotham at Piercebridge on 1 December. He was then attacked by Lord Fairfax at Tadcaster but utterly defeated him, driving a wedge into the Parliamentary forces in Yorkshire. He next captured Pontefract castle and Newark in order to keep the route from the north to Oxford open. These victories were offset, however, when in January 1643 Lord Fairfax's son, Sir Thomas, probably the ablest commander on the Parliamentary side, captured Bradford, Leeds and Wakefield and Lord Newcastle was obliged to fall back on York, leaving a garrison in Newark which remained Royalist to the end of the war.

On 5 December Goring had appeared again, this time in a naval role but incompetently in this element, when he unsuccessfully attacked three Parliamentary men-of-war, lost several of his own ships and returned to Newcastle. Early in January 1643 the Queen returned from her mission abroad with large quantities of stores and munitions, although two transports of horses were lost in a storm. At the end of March Sir Hugh Cholmley, governor of Scarborough for the Puritans, deserted them and joined the Royalist cause, delivering Scarborough castle to the King in the process. The Hothams appear to have had like ideas, but as yet did not follow Cholmley's lead although they did all they could to thwart the Fairfaxes, whom they disliked, and the latter retreated into Leeds where they were besieged.

In the northwest Sir William Brereton worsted a Royalist force at Nantwich on 28 January and penetrated into the Midlands. He did so without much success because by the end of February the Royalists had seized Lichfield, Tamworth, Stafford, Stratford and Ashby de la Zouche, thereby opening another route from the north to Oxford. On 30 March Lord George Goring, back in the saddle, came up against Sir Thomas Fairfax in Yorkshire, and with a very inferior number of horse fell upon him on Seacroft Moor. After a brisk fight Sir Thomas was routed with over 1,000 casualties. Parliament was worried and Lord Brooke was sent to the area. He recaptured Stafford and early in March regained Lichfield, although he was killed in the battle.

The King now sent Lord Northampton north from Oxford and he successfully attacked the Parliamentary forces at Hopton Heath, two miles from Stafford, but was killed in the fray. His body was captured and prevented from being buried by being held as a 'hostage' by the Parliamentarians under Brereton. As a result Prince Rupert was ordered to take over the Royalist forces in the Midlands; he sacked the intensely Puritan small town of Birmingham on 3 April, and after heavy fighting reoccupied Lichfield on 21 April.

Despite these successes, Charles's position in Oxford was getting dangerous for want of munitions with which to defend the city if it were attacked. However, the Queen, still in the north, dispatched a large convoy of arms and ammunition to him which reached Woodstock on 13 May, and the situation was saved.

MAP 7

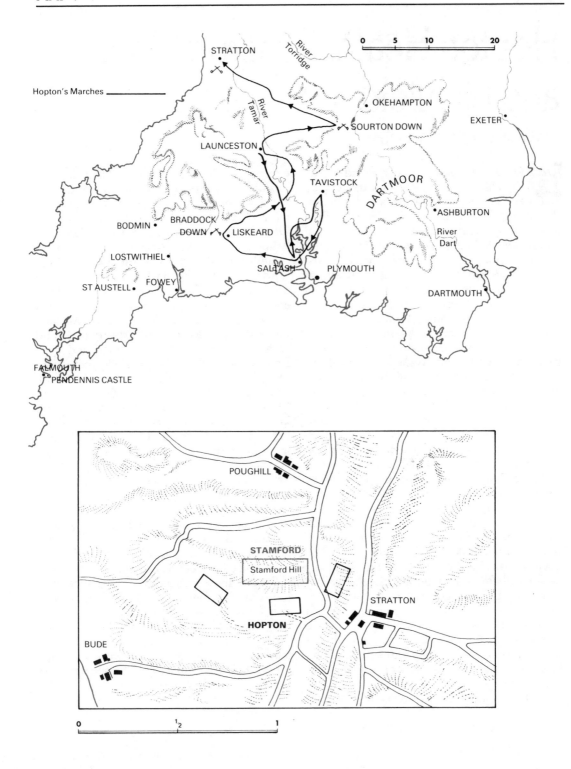

MAP 7

The Southwest and the Battle of Stratton

October 1642–21 May 1643

IN CORNWALL Sir Ralph Hopton, now Lieutenant General of the Horse in the west, soon gained the support of a great leader of the county, Sir Bevil Grenville, the grandson of Sir Richard Grenville of *Revenge* fame. With the Trained Bands and the county militia he quickly occupied Launceston and Saltash and cleared the Parliamentarians from the county, but now he faced problems as the Cornish Trained Bands would not cross the boundary into Devon, which to them was almost a foreign country. The solution was found in raising, with Sir Bevil's help, five regiments of foot and one of horse from volunteers, which in fact probably included many of the Trained Bands. He soon had a sizeable army under his command and in November 1642 crossed the border, occupied Tavistock and threatened Plymouth.

The people of Devon mostly sided with the Puritans and so Hopton, without support, soon had to retreat into Cornwall, whence he was followed by Ruthen, the Parliamentary commander of Plymouth. On 19 January Hopton attacked Ruthen and the new Puritan commander in the west, the Earl of Stamford, who was advancing on Bodmin, at Braddock Down near Liskeard; he routed them with many prisoners being taken. Just before this victory Hopton had had a great stroke of luck when a large Parliamentary fleet was driven into Falmouth by a gale and seized under the guns of Pendennis castle. From these ships he gained large quantities of arms and money.

Hopton now crossed into Devon again, with Stamford in rapid retreat. His expedition was short-lived because at the end of February Stamford suddenly turned and drove him back into Cornwall.

On 23 April Hopton attacked General James Chudleigh on Beacon Hill and around Polston Bridge near Launceston, but followed up his success too closely and without proper reconnaissance or precautions, and was surprised and defeated two days later at Sourton Down. Stamford, seizing his opportunity, now attacked into Cornwall in strength. He sent Sir George Chudleigh, father of James, to occupy Bodmin and concentrated the rest of his force at Stratton, near the modern resort of Bude, in the only Puritan part of the county. Hearing of these movements Hopton marched to Stratton and, in spite of inferiority of numbers — about 3,000 as against 6,500 — decided to attack without delay on 16 May while the Parliamentary army was still divided.

Stamford's army was positioned on an irregular ridge on top of a steep hill, later named after him, which was nearly impregnable, and was well supplied with arms and cannon. Hopton attacked him there with four columns from different directions, holding his cavalry in reserve and relying on the advice of Sir Bevil Grenville who lived nearby and knew every inch of the country.

The fighting was extremely heavy and finally, running short of ammunition and having had little success so far, Hopton ordered an attack with pike and sword as a last supreme effort. The Cornishmen surged up the hill and eventually stood on top of it — although the enemy was still on the heights — and turned the enemy's own cannon on them. James Chudleigh was captured during a counter-attack, and the Parliamentary army, attacked in the flank, broke and fled, leaving many dead and prisoners behind. It was accompanied, or possibly preceded, by Stamford.

MAP 8

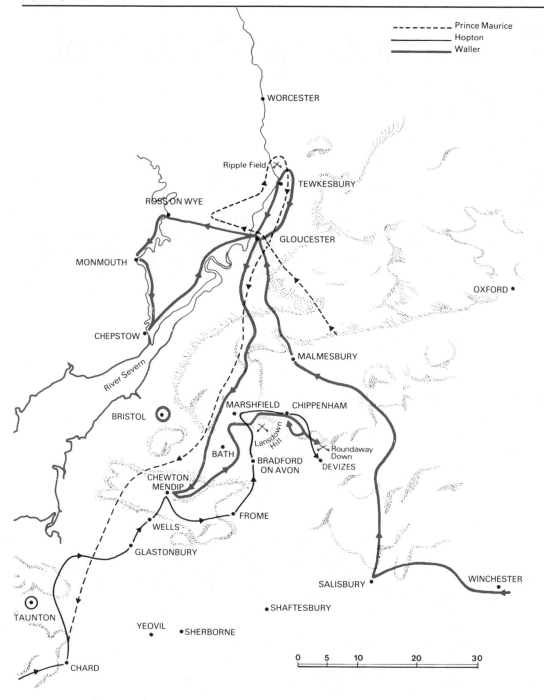

Prince Maurice
Hopton
Waller

WORCESTER

Ripple Field

TEWKESBURY

ROSS ON WYE

GLOUCESTER

MONMOUTH

OXFORD

CHEPSTOW

River Severn

MALMESBURY

BRISTOL

MARSHFIELD

CHIPPENHAM

BATH

Lansdown Hill

Roundaway Down

BRADFORD ON AVON

DEVIZES

CHEWTON MENDIP

FROME

WELLS

GLASTONBURY

SALISBURY

WINCHESTER

TAUNTON

SHAFTESBURY

YEOVIL

SHERBORNE

0   5   10   20   30

CHARD

MAP 8

Ripple Field and Chewton Mendip

9 March–3 July 1643

MEANWHILE in the southwest Prince Rupert had, on 9 March, attempted to capture the valuable prize of Bristol, but a plot to open the gates for him had failed and he was forced to retire again to Oxford. Bristol was secured by Sir William Waller six days later. Waller had been appointed Parliamentary commander in the southern counties, although he was at daggers drawn with Essex. He captured Winchester, destroying Lord Grandison's horse in the engagement, and on 21 March he took Malmesbury. Three days later he seized Gloucester, and then exploited farther west to Ross-on-Wye, Monmouth and Chepstow.

This threat was too much for the Royalists to accept quietly and Prince Maurice was sent to attack Waller in the rear. Learning of this, and in hostile country, Waller withdrew to Gloucester and undertook an expedition to Tewkesbury where he destroyed Prince Maurice's bridge of boats across the River Severn. Maurice, caught on the wrong side of the river, marched northwards and crossed the river at Upton bridge, where Waller tried to cut him off. But he had not reckoned with Maurice's speed of movement and the armies met at Ripple Field, three miles north of Tewkesbury where on 13 April Waller was routed.

After the battle of Stratton, George Chudleigh had retreated from Bodmin and his son James changed sides, so impressed was he with his erstwhile enemies. There was now no Parliamentary force of any size left in Devon, and Hopton moved rapidly and secured the county, with the exception of the garrison towns of Exeter, Plymouth, Dartmouth, Bideford and Barnstaple. Essex was thoroughly alarmed. Hopton then joined forces with Prince Maurice and the Marquess of Hertford, the problem of command being solved by Hopton being given operational command while Hertford retained overall command. Prince Maurice commanded the horse, who were good fighting men, but they were ill-disciplined and so fond of plundering as to be an unruly robber band treating Royalist and Parliamentary supporters without distinction.

The King's intention was to assemble a strong army around Oxford with which to crush Essex and Waller using interior lines of communication to advantage. The joint Royalist army put a garrison into Taunton and moved on to Wells, in which area Waller had established himself in the Mendip Hills to defend the approaches to Bath. Five miles farther on, on 10 June, they reached the small village of Chewton Mendip and encountered Waller's outposts. Lord Carnarvon's horse advanced but met with strong resistance and, being tired from their long march, retreated in disarray, during which fray Prince Maurice was wounded and taken prisoner. Another small body of Cavalier horse took over, advanced in the evening mist and routed the Roundhead regiments, releasing Prince Maurice in the process. Nevertheless it was an indecisive action.

Both armies reached the area of Bath, where they manoeuvred for position. It was at this point that Hopton, who was an old comrade in arms and friend of Waller, wrote to him and suggested a private meeting to discuss the situation. Waller replied to the effect that they had chosen their own sides and that such a meeting would be dishonourable. In spite of friendships of the past the war could now only be decided by the sword, so great were the differences of outlook.

MAP 9

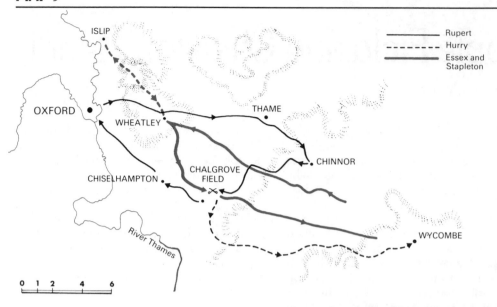

John Hampden (1594-1643)

Hampden was a politician rather than a soldier. Born in Buckinghamshire, a cousin of Cromwell, he was MP for Wendover and made his fame due to his refusal to pay Ship Money. Originally a moderate in Parliament, he became a strong Parliamentary supporter after his arrest in 1642. He raised an infantry regiment for the Roundheads but, fighting with the cavalry, was mortally wounded at Chalgrove Field and died at Thame. His death was regarded as a great loss to the country.

MAP 9

The Battle of Chalgrove Field

13 April–3 July 1643

O N 13 April Essex had advanced with a large army of about 19,000 men from Windsor towards Reading, captured a Royalist post on Caversham Hill and laid siege to the city. The garrison of Reading was weak, and the defences, although reasonably strong, could not be fully manned. Although Rupert and the King advanced from Oxford to meet Essex, the commander, Colonel Fielding, having taken over from Sir Arthur Aston when he was badly wounded, had already offered to surrender. There was nothing that Charles could do and the garrison was allowed to march out with the honours of war.

In June the two main armies were between London and Oxford and Essex decided to make a show of force against the Oxford defences. By 13 June his advance guard was at Wheatley, but a detachment of 2,500 men which had been sent against a Royalist force at Islip decided that discretion was the better part of valour and retreated without a shot being fired. Prince Rupert, having returned from Lichfield, now learned through a deserter from the Puritan army, Colonel Hurry, that a convoy was on its way to Thame with money for Essex's army; always being prepared to take any chance of a successful action, he moved with a select body of some 1,700 men, mostly cavalry, to intercept it.

A party of his men surprised a small party of Roundheads at Chinnor and annihilated them, but unfortunately the noise of the fray had warned the convoy which went into hiding in the woods. Having been deprived of his prey Rupert set off back to Oxford, but by now Roundhead troops under Sir Philip Stapleton were heading to cut off his withdrawal. Learning of this Rupert moved quickly on 18 June, posting his foot at Chiselhampton bridge to guard his line of retreat and deploying his horse at Chalgrove Field three miles east of the bridge.

The Roundheads were drawn up behind a hedge and Rupert attacked them. The Puritans put up a stubborn defence but the odds were against them and eventually they broke and were routed. This time Rupert did not give chase, but, realising that Essex could soon follow up with a major force, returned to Oxford. The conflict itself was relatively unimportant except for one factor; John Hampden, who was with the Roundhead force as a volunteer while waiting for his own regiment to arrive, was wounded in the battle and died six days later at Thame.

Essex's army was now in some disorder, partly from his own dilatoriness and partly from sickness due to the bad weather, and he abandoned his foray against Oxford. On 25 June a detachment of cavalry under Colonel Hurry, who had been knighted for his services before Chalgrove Field, swept round the rear of the Parliamentary army, defeated Sir Philip Stapleton's horse and plundered Wycombe. This created alarm in London and, fearing an attack, the defences were manned.

In the west on 3 July the Royalists under Hopton made the first move near Bath. Their aim was not to capture the city but to join up with the main army at Oxford, which was the King's intention, tying down Waller in the process. They swept though Bradford-on-Avon, brushing aside Waller's patrols and an ambush, so cutting Waller off from London. However, being unable to draw him far from his defences at Bath, they moved round to the north of the city towards Lansdown Hill, a long, high, steep ridge which appeared to be an easier line of approach and dominated the city (see Map 8).

MAP 10

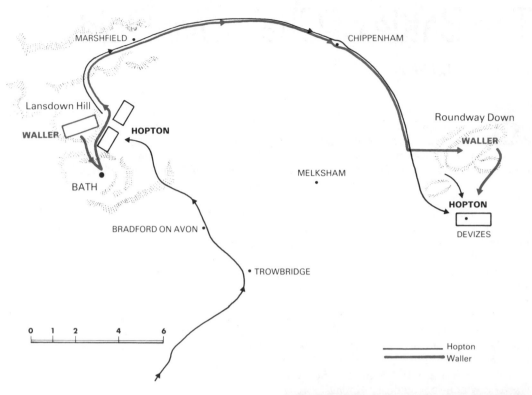

MARSHFIELD

CHIPPENHAM

Lansdown Hill

Roundway Down

WALLER

HOPTON

WALLER

BATH

MELKSHAM

HOPTON

DEVIZES

BRADFORD ON AVON

TROWBRIDGE

0 1 2 4 6

——— Hopton
——— Waller

Sir Bevil Grenville (1596-1643)

Born in Cornwall, he was grandson of Sir Richard
Grenville of the *Revenge*. He loved learning and was an
enlightened landowner. Initially opposed to the King, he
later joined him and was the leading Royalist in the
southwest. His death in the battle of Lansdown was a great
loss to the Royalist cause.

MAP 10

The Battles of Lansdown and Roundway Down

3–24 July 1643

WALLER also appreciated that the ridge of Lansdown Hill was the key to the city of Bath. The Royalists soon found that he did not intend to give up his control of the ridge without a struggle and that the hill was strongly defended with breastworks, and they retreated a short way. On 5 July Waller attacked the Cavaliers with Sir Arthur Hazlerigg's newly formed regiment of horse, but although the charge was initially successful the strength of the enemy horse was too great and he returned to Lansdown again.

As at Stratton, Hopton's Cornishmen now attacked the heights, making great use of flank attacks. At first they were protected by woods; and Grenville's regiment, on the road with the horse, was protected by the steepness of the hill and by a bend in the road. Eventually the whole force came out into the open and a desperate battle ensued.

Five times the Parliamentary horse charged down the slopes, but in vain. Nevertheless, the Royalist cavalry suffered very heavy casualties, and it has been said that many of them actually left the field and fled to Oxford, spreading alarm and despondency. Finally the Cavalier force surged forward and overwhelmed Waller's position, but in the victory came sadness because Sir Bevil Grenville was killed in the thick of the fighting. During the night Waller retreated to Bath, but the Royalist army had been too heavily mauled to take up the pursuit and was too weak to put Bath to siege. Also, Hopton was badly injured the following day when an ammunition cart blew up.

The Royalists retired through Marshfield to Chippenham, where they spent two days, and finally to Devizes, with Waller heavily attacking their rear. But the Royalists were still too strong for him to do much damage, and although he captured a convoy of ammunition, Waller was unable to prevent the Cavalier horse escaping towards Oxford and Salisbury.

In spite of his injury Hopton was with his army in Devizes and was still able to command his force. Waller first took up a position on Roundway Down overlooking Devizes on 10 July and then descended and laid siege to the town; although the Royalists were in superior numbers the town was unfortified and incapable of being held for long.

Waller decided to attack the town on 13 July. Before he could do so Prince Maurice returned to the battle reinforced by Lord Wilmot's horse and established himself in his turn on Roundway Down, which Waller had inexplicably relinquished. Waller ordered them to be removed and Hazlerigg attempted to charge uphill at them. He was heavily repulsed, and the whole of the Roundhead cavalry fled precipitately downhill again, where it joined up with Waller's foot.

Hopton's men now sallied forth from the town and attacked Waller in the rear, and with Maurice's and Wilmot's cavalry attacking downhill Waller was in an impossible position. Casualties were very heavy, many prisoners were taken and Waller's army was virtually annihilated and for practical purposes ceased to exist — as a result Waller was also deprived of the opportunity to take over command of the Roundhead armies from Essex. This gave the Royalists the platform that they needed for destroying all Parliamentary power in the west.

MAP 11

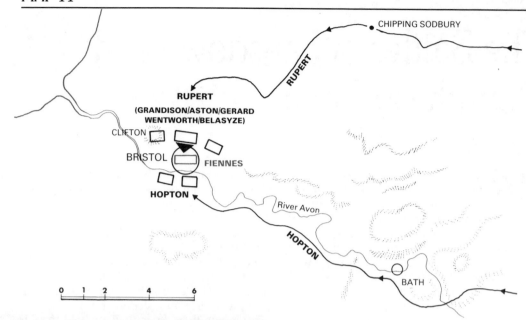

Ralph, Lord Hopton (1598-1652)

A Somerset man, after studying at Oxford he served abroad for a while. He was MP for Wells but joined the King and raised the Cornish army. He was one of the most brilliant Royalist commanders, being a firm disciplinarian who had the devotion of his troops and was respected by both sides. He surrendered at Truro in 1646. Being excepted from pardon he remained in exile, dying at Bruges.

MAP 11

The Capture of Bristol

25–27 July 1643

THE two major Parliamentary garrisons were at Bristol and Gloucester, and the capture of these cities became an immediate requirement for the Royalists, the former because of its port facilities and the latter because it controlled the Severn valley and the crossings into Wales. Prince Rupert, with three brigades of foot under Lord Grandison (who was Colonel General of Foot), Henry Wentworth and John Belasyze, and two regiments of horse under Sir Arthur Aston (recovered from his wound at Reading) and Charles Gerard, moved out from Oxford to join up with Hopton's Cornish army.

Waller had retired to Gloucester after Roundway Down and Rupert decided to attack Bristol first, cutting Waller off from that city. In fact Waller, with very few troops left, did not remain and marched to Evesham and eventually to London. Rupert marched through Chipping Sodbury and then to the northwest of Bristol and established a strong post on Clifton Hill. The defences of the city were in two rings with forts on all the major hills, although many of the works were incomplete; and the Parliamentary commander, Nathaniel Fiennes, a brave man who had fought at Powick Bridge, had a quite insufficient force to hold the city. Nevertheless Bristol was strongly for Parliament, despite a considerable Royalist faction, and Fiennes hoped he could rely on a mass of armed citizens to help in its defence.

Rupert massed the Cornish army on the southern approaches to the city whilst he himself remained on the northern side, and called upon Fiennes to surrender, which he of course refused to do. After considering the pros and cons of investment or assault Rupert decided on the latter and launched his attack on the morning of 26 July. The Cornishmen attacked gallantly but could not penetrate the defences, suffering very heavy casualties and

several of their commanders being killed. Rupert meanwhile had managed to find a weakly held gap in the defences on his front and, beating off counter-attacks, fed his cavalry through into the city; they were led by Henry Washington, great uncle of George Washington the first President of the United States.

The Roundheads defended strongly in the centre of Bristol but were eventually overwhelmed and Fiennes surrendered. Not only was the city a great prize, but there were a number of Royalist armed merchantmen confined in the harbour and these were immediately put ready for sea under Sir John Pennington. Parliament was alarmed and ordered a fleet to assemble in the mouth of the Severn. Fiennes was courtmartialled and sentenced to death for dereliction of duty; Essex commuted the sentence but Fiennes was removed from further active service.

At this point the animosity between Rupert and the other leading Royalist commanders, which had been smouldering for a long time, burst into flame. Hertford had been appointed Lord Lieutenant of the counties around Bristol and regarded Rupert, who had brought the troops from Oxford, as under his command. Rupert, however, had signed the capitulation terms for Bristol without consulting Hertford and the latter, to show his authority, appointed Hopton as governor of the city. Rupert wrote to the King asking for the post for himself and Charles, ignorant of the facts, granted this to him. Hertford was furious and Charles went to Bristol to try to pour oil on the troubled waters. Hopton, anxious to prevent further strife, offered to become Lieutenant Governor under Rupert, but the King took Hertford and Hopton to Oxford with him, ostensibly to consult them on the conduct of the war, and raised Hopton to the peerage.

MAP 12

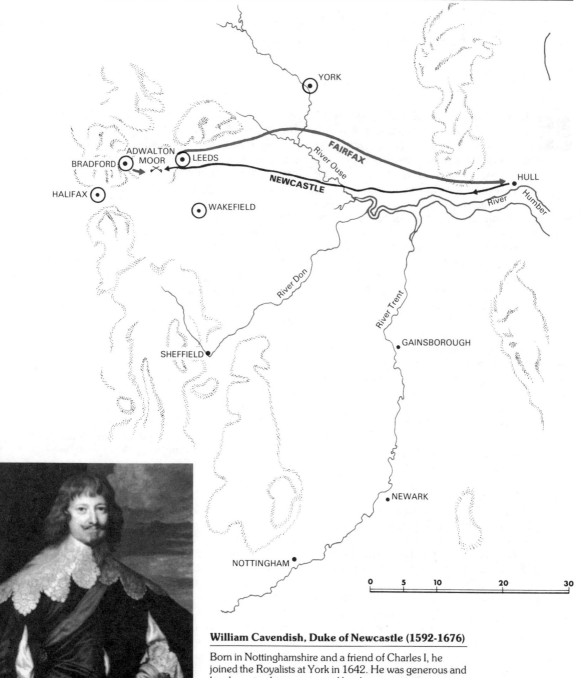

YORK

BRADFORD

ADWALTON
MOOR

LEEDS

FAIRFAX

River Ouse

NEWCASTLE

HALIFAX

WAKEFIELD

HULL

River Humber

River Don

River Trent

GAINSBOROUGH

SHEFFIELD

NEWARK

NOTTINGHAM

| 0 | 5 | 10 | 20 | 30 |

William Cavendish, Duke of Newcastle (1592-1676)

Born in Nottinghamshire and a friend of Charles I, he joined the Royalists at York in 1642. He was generous and loyal, wrote plays, poetry and books on equitation, was a fine swordsman, and a brave and competent commander. He despaired for the Royalist cause after Marston Moor and left the country, which damaged his reputation. He returned after the Restoration to re-establish his estates, ruined during his service to the King.
National Portrait Gallery

MAP 12

The Action at Adwalton Moor

2 June–13 July 1643

MEANWHILE, early in June, it appeared that Cromwell's hope of producing a large enough force in the north Midlands to rescue the Fairfaxes from Lord Newcastle in Yorkshire was to be realised. A force of some 6,000 men under Lords Grey and Willoughby, Cromwell, Hotham and others assembled at Nottingham, but unfortunately for him a strong body of Royalists appeared in the area: Cromwell's support evaporated rapidly and his hopes were dashed.

Sir Thomas Fairfax was still in difficulties. Hotham's earlier thoughts of desertion now became known and he was arrested and imprisoned in Nottingham castle, Sir John Meldrum taking over command of all forces there. Hotham escaped, contacted the Queen at Newark and set off to join his father at Hull with the intention of delivering the port to the Royalists. But the Mayor of Hull gained information of his intents and whereabouts, put the defence of Hull into the hands of the citizens and arrested Hotham. He and his father were sent to London.

If Hull had been taken by the Royalists the Parliamentary cause in the north would have been doomed. Even without this the Roundheads still had grave problems. Newcastle now gathered his army for a final attack on the Fairfaxes in Yorkshire and marched to Bradford. Sir Thomas knew that he could not survive a siege and marched out with a force of only 4,000 men to oppose Newcastle's 10,000. On 30 June they advanced along the ridge of Adwalton Moor and found Newcastle coming in the opposite direction. Battle was joined and although for a time it seemed that Thomas Fairfax's skill would prevail he was eventually overwhelmed by sheer strength of numbers, his left wing was broken and he was driven off the hill. The army retreated in disarray to Bradford to await the end.

At that point a messenger arrived at Bradford from Hull, telling him of what had transpired there and asking for Lord Fairfax to come and take over command of the port. The elder Fairfax departed immediately, and Thomas Fairfax, left in Bradford for a while, escaped the besiegers, leaving his family behind as prisoners, and also set out for Hull. Lord Fairfax had already been installed as governor when Thomas arrived, and the two Fairfaxes together prepared to defend the city. But all of Yorkshire, except for Hull, was now in Newcastle's hands, because with the loss of Bradford the other major towns of Leeds, Halifax and Wakefield were abandoned.

On 3 July the Queen set out from Newark for Oxford. Essex had left Thame and established himself at Aylesbury, but if he had any ideas of intercepting the Queen they were dashed by Rupert, who swept around his army, attacking where he could but avoiding any decisive action — much to Essex's disgust. Rupert met the Queen at Stratford to escort her and on 13 July Charles and Henrietta Maria were reunited at Edgehill. From there they rode into Oxford, the Queen bringing with her reinforcements of 1,000 horse, 2,000 foot and large supplies of arms and ammunition (see Map 2).

MAP 13

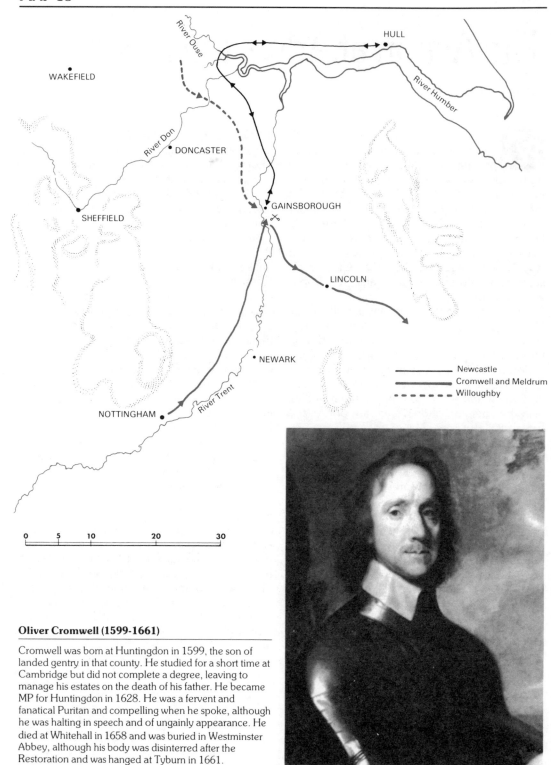

WAKEFIELD

River Ouse

HULL

River Humber

River Don

DONCASTER

SHEFFIELD

GAINSBOROUGH

LINCOLN

NEWARK

	Newcastle
	Cromwell and Meldrum
----	Willoughby

NOTTINGHAM

River Trent

| 0 | 5 | 10 | 20 | 30 |

Oliver Cromwell (1599-1661)

Cromwell was born at Huntingdon in 1599, the son of
landed gentry in that county. He studied for a short time at
Cambridge but did not complete a degree, leaving to
manage his estates on the death of his father. He became
MP for Huntingdon in 1628. He was a fervent and
fanatical Puritan and compelling when he spoke, although
he was halting in speech and of ungainly appearance. He
died at Whitehall in 1658 and was buried in Westminster
Abbey, although his body was disinterred after the
Restoration and was hanged at Tyburn in 1661.

MAP 13

The Action at Gainsborough

20 July–10 August 1643

ON 20 July Lord Willoughby, having moved southwards, had captured Gainsborough and was being threatened by a strong body of Royalist horse under Charles Cavendish, a kinsman of Newcastle. Cromwell and Sir John Meldrum, with a larger force than Cavendish's, moved to support Willoughby. They knew full well that Newcastle would have to pass through the town, having left Hull under siege and being on the march towards London, and on 28 July they came up against Cavendish's horse on a hill just south of Gainsborough. They reached the summit of the hill and charged Cavendish, routing his cavalry and pursuing them as had Rupert at Edgehill. Cromwell suddenly realised that Cavendish had kept one regiment in reserve which was about to attack the unwary victors and, rallying his troop, attacked Cavendish from behind, driving him headlong down the hill. Cavendish was killed in the battle.

News now arrived that a small Royalist force was approaching and the Roundhead commanders went out to meet it, only to find that the 'small force' was in fact Newcastle's complete army. Willoughby's men fled, but Meldrum's and Cromwell's cavalry fought a brilliant rearguard action back into Gainsborough. The whole action at Gainsborough was really only a skirmish, but it gave a hint of things to come, that the Roundheads had at last formed a cavalry force as strong as the Royalist one under Rupert. Cromwell realised that he could not defend Gainsborough against Newcastle and rode off, the town surrendering on 30 July.

Parliament now appointed the Earl of Manchester as Major General and commander of the armies of the associated counties of the east Midlands, with the task of blocking Newcastle's march towards London. At the same time Waller was reinstated and placed in command of a new army of 11,000 men to oppose the army of Lord Carnarvon and Prince Maurice and to prevent it approaching from the west. The main Parliamentary army of Essex was still given the task of countering the main Royalist army under the King.

Newcastle's hopes of a march southwards were foiled; not by the enemy, but as Hopton's march had been earlier, because his troops, mostly recruited in Yorkshire, refused to move far from the county whilst Hull was still in Roundhead hands, and thus their own houses and lands were in danger of forays from the port. Newcastle was therefore forced to return to the siege of Hull and to try everything he could to capture the town. It can be said of Plymouth in the west and Hull in the north, that their determined resistance for the Parliamentary cause saved Parliament and enabled the Roundheads eventually to win the war.

MAP 14

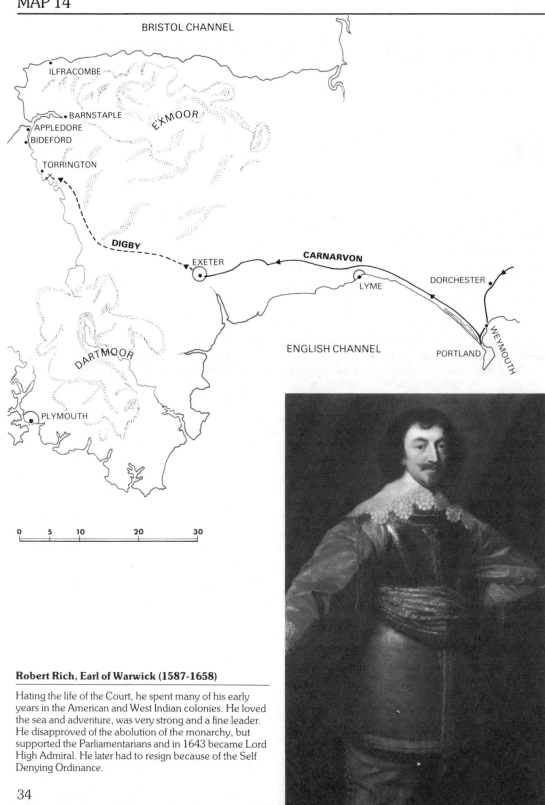

BRISTOL CHANNEL

ILFRACOMBE

BARNSTAPLE

EXMOOR

APPLEDORE

BIDEFORD

TORRINGTON

DIGBY

EXETER

CARNARVON

DORCHESTER

LYME

DARTMOOR

ENGLISH CHANNEL

PORTLAND

WEYMOUTH

PLYMOUTH

0 5 10 20 30

Robert Rich, Earl of Warwick (1587-1658)

Hating the life of the Court, he spent many of his early
years in the American and West Indian colonies. He loved
the sea and adventure, was very strong and a fine leader.
He disapproved of the abolition of the monarchy, but
supported the Parliamentarians and in 1643 became Lord
High Admiral. He later had to resign because of the Self
Denying Ordinance.

MAP 14

The Southwest and Torrington

4 August–4 September 1643

THE Roundheads appeared to be in serious trouble in the southwest, and probably the King should have mounted an attack on London jointly by the southern armies and Newcastle. But the country's outlook was still very parochial, and men who were prepared to fight hard to free their own counties were not always so keen to move farther afield; additionally, the Cornish army had suffered severe casualties at Bristol. Furthermore, Plymouth and the southern ports and Gloucester were still strongly held by Parliament, and there had been some infiltration back into Devon and Cornwall by the Roundheads, which would have left a sizeable force in Charles's rear.

The Earl of Carnarvon, supported by Prince Maurice, was ordered to march to Dorchester, which soon surrendered on 4 August, followed by Weymouth and Portland. However, he failed to press his advantage and take Lyme Regis and Poole while their morale was low. Carnarvon had gained support for the Royalists by his generous treatment of the towns he had taken, but unfortunately this action was negated by Maurice's 'robber bands' which alienated many Royalist supporters by plundering the captured towns.

Maurice now moved to Exeter which was being besieged by Sir John Berkeley. The Parliamentary fleet under the Earl of Warwick attempted to relieve the town but failed, losing three ships, and the Roundheads decided to raise the siege by land, using the garrisons of Plymouth, Bideford and Barnstaple. Colonel John Digby was therefore sent into north Devon to try to prevent the junction of the force from Bideford and Barnstaple, and having reached Torrington on 21 August learned of an impending attack.

He positioned his small force, but there was no sign of the expected Roundhead advance and he dismissed his troops. Hearing shortly afterwards that the enemy was approaching after all, he ordered his foot to take up positions to defend the streets of the town while he rode out with a body of horse, which he posted in the various woods and hedgerows to ambush the Roundheads.

Digby then saw a small party of Roundhead musketeers approaching down the road and, gathering the few officers near him, charged them. The enemy broke and fled, and, communicating their panic, the whole Roundhead force broke, hotly pursued by the Cavaliers. As a result of this extraordinary fray, Appledore, Barnstaple and Bideford surrendered, and it is doubtful if a charge by six horsemen can often have had such momentous success as this did. Dismayed, the Roundheads now surrendered Exeter on 4 September and the Royalist cause at this point probably reached its high water mark.

Parliament now did not just appear to be in serious trouble in the southwest, but was in desperate trouble.

MAP 15

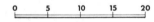

Sir William Waller (1598-1668)

A Kentish man, before the war he was an MP and a close friend of Hopton. He joined the Parliamentarians and next to Fairfax was probably their best general, and a good tactician. It was he, and not Cromwell, who proposed the formation of the New Model Army, but underestimated, he resigned his command in 1645. Later accused of conspiracy, he escaped to Holland but later returned to England.

MAP 15

The Relief of Gloucester and Aldbourne Chase

10 August–19 September 1643

ON 10 August Charles moved his Oxford army to Gloucester. When his demand for the surrender of the city was refused he settled down to besiege it, Prince Rupert's advice to storm it as at Bristol having been rejected. In hindsight this was his major strategic error of the war, tying up a large army in a siege when it could have been used to bring Essex's army to battle.

Parliament fully realised the importance of Gloucester and made every effort to raise the siege. Essex assembled an army at Hounslow and set off on a hazardous expedition across country occupied by the Royalist army, which could have destroyed him if it had acted with any resolve. As Essex marched through Bicester and Stow-on-the-Wold both Wilmot and Rupert harried his flanks but did not press their attacks, and on 5 September Essex reached the outskirts of Gloucester unscathed. Charles chose not to fight Essex with the Gloucester garrison behind his own army and raised the siege. Essex entered the city on 8 September just in time, as the defenders were almost out of supplies and ammunition.

Having improved the defences of Gloucester and resupplied it, Essex set off back to London, this time taking a route south of the Oxford defences. But first, to confuse the King he marched to Tewkesbury and Pershore. He stayed there for a few days, making cavalry forays into the countryside, and then, taking advantage of a very dark night, marched rapidly southwards to Cirencester where by chance he was able to capture a Royalist supply train.

By now, after a period of conjecture, Charles realised what was happening and moved to intercept Essex. Rupert, who was determined to prevent Essex reaching London, and was looking for a major battle to win the war, came upon the Roundhead army at Aldbourne Chase on 18 September and attacked it. The fight was brief but sharp, and although the result was inconclusive — since Rupert's force was not strong enough to achieve anything more at this stage — it slowed down Essex's march.

Essex decided to put the River Kennet between himself and the Royalist army and made for Newbury. The tired Parliamentary army entered Hungerford on a wet and windy night, but having found little shelter for the cold and hungry troops, Essex continued towards Newbury where, in a town with strong Parliamentary leanings, he hoped to find dry billets. But the delay at Aldbourne had enabled the Cavalier army to get to Newbury ahead of him, and to insert itself between him and London.

As Essex marched on towards Newbury his advance guard was again attacked by Rupert's horse. Newbury being denied to it, his army had to spend the night in the open in the pouring rain. With his positional advantage the King, on 19 September, deployed his army. Behind him, but far enough away to pose little threat, was Waller's army of 4,000 men, although Charles did not realise that Waller was not keen to endanger his own army to help Essex. Essex probably wished to slip past the Royalists without a battle, but the ground was marshy to the south and it would have been a very dangerous manoeuvre.

MAP 16

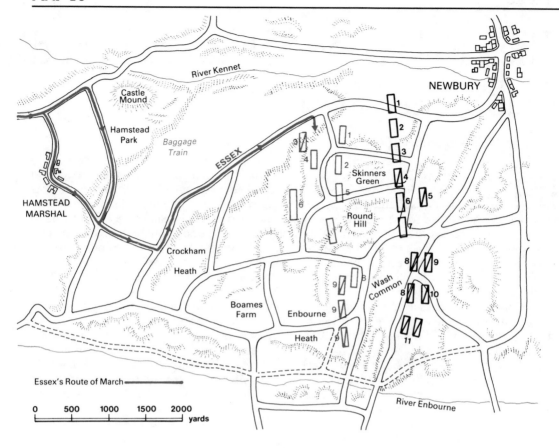

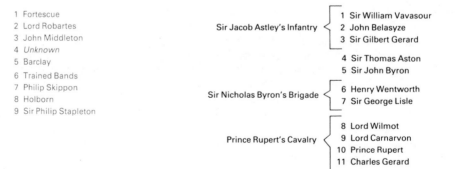

1 Fortescue
2 Lord Robartes
3 John Middleton
4 *Unknown*
5 Barclay
6 Trained Bands
7 Philip Skippon
8 Holborn
9 Sir Philip Stapleton

Sir Jacob Astley's Infantry
1 Sir William Vavasour
2 John Belasyze
3 Sir Gilbert Gerard

4 Sir Thomas Aston
5 Sir John Byron

Sir Nicholas Byron's Brigade
6 Henry Wentworth
7 Sir George Lisle

Prince Rupert's Cavalry
8 Lord Wilmot
9 Lord Carnarvon
10 Prince Rupert
11 Charles Gerard

MAP 16

The First Battle of Newbury (1)

20 September 1643

ON 19 September the King deployed his army mainly to the north and east of Skinner's Green, with cavalry patrols on the ridge by Wash Farm, but for some inexplicable reason he failed to occupy the dominant feature of Round Hill, which was to cause problems later. (Little of the ground can now be seen as much of it has been built over.) The numbers involved were probably as at Edgehill, about 14,000 on each side, with the King superior in horse and each side having about 20 guns.

The Cavalier horse was commanded by Prince Rupert, with brigades under Lords Carnarvon and Wilmot, Rupert, Sir John Byron, Charles Gerard and Sir Thomas Aston. Sir Jacob Astley was in command of the infantry, with Sir Nicholas Byron, Sir William Vavasour, Sir Gilbert Gerard and John Balasyze as his brigade commanders. There were four brigades of Roundhead foot, each of three regiments, plus the Trained Bands (who were probably the best trained men in the field in either army) in reserve, and two brigades of cavalry under Sir Philip Stapleton and John Middleton. Essex personally commanded the Parliamentary right wing and Skippon the left wing and the reserves.

The King's army deployed slowly, perhaps through overconfidence, and at the start of the battle Skippon occupied Round Hill with infantry and placed artillery on it. The Royalists found that as their positions were overlooked, they would have to dislodge the Roundheads from the high ground. Nevertheless, the Parliamentary baggage train was in Hamstead Park, and the Royalists opposite it on their right wing had a strong advantage until Skippon moved part of Lord Robartes'

brigade and Fortescue's regiment to protect the area.

Round Hill was broken up into small fields with many high hedges, and the attack on it was made by Sir John Byron's cavalry and his uncle Nicholas' brigade of foot. Because the country was difficult the infantry soon became bogged down, and the battle raged among the hedgerows with many casualties. Sir Nicholas asked for cavalry support, but even though the ground was even more difficult for cavalry, they attacked the hill and succeeded in getting a foothold on it. They came across the Roundhead infantry defending a high hedge with a gap in it only large enough for one horse at a time to pass through. While giving orders for the gap to be widened Sir John Byron's horse was shot, and while he was getting another one Lord Falkland galloped through the gap alone and was killed. (It is said that he died deliberately because of his distress at the disaster of the war.) Byron's regiments assaulted again but the musket fire was too intense and they withdrew in some confusion.

Later in the day another assault was made and this time Byron's and Aston's regiments drove the enemy from the summit, but were again halted by heavy fire from behind another hedge. Skippon now changed his position and brought up the Trained Bands, and thus a third cavalry charge, whilst routing the enemy from the hill, could achieve little further progress against the determined infantry. The cavalry suffered heavily but fought very gallantly, and the Royalist infantry was left to hold the hill while the battered horse withdrew.

MAP 17

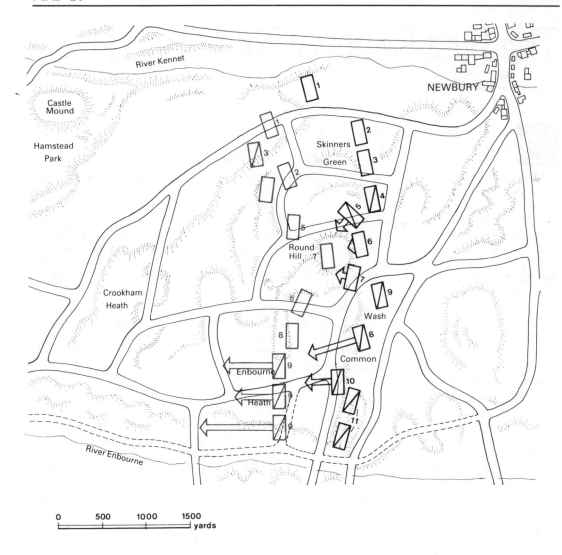

River Kennet

Castle Mound

Hamstead Park

Skinners Green

NEWBURY

Round Hill

Crookham Heath

Wash

Common

Enbourne

Heath

River Enbourne

```
0      500     1000    1500
|---|---|---|---|---|---| yards
```

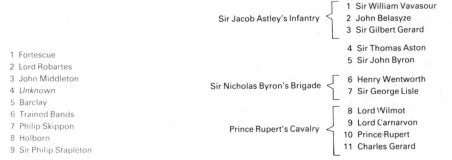

1 Fortescue
2 Lord Robartes
3 John Middleton
4 *Unknown*
5 Barclay
6 Trained Bands
7 Philip Skippon
8 Holborn
9 Sir Philip Stapleton

Sir Jacob Astley's Infantry
1 Sir William Vavasour
2 John Belasyze
3 Sir Gilbert Gerard

4 Sir Thomas Aston
5 Sir John Byron

Sir Nicholas Byron's Brigade
6 Henry Wentworth
7 Sir George Lisle

Prince Rupert's Cavalry
8 Lord Wilmot
9 Lord Carnarvon
10 Prince Rupert
11 Charles Gerard

MAP 17

The First Battle of Newbury (2)

20 September 1643

THE fight now switched to the ridge above Wash Farm and the area south and east of it, where it continued ferociously for the rest of the day. Rupert charged Stapleton's horse, which was supported by some of the Trained Bands, and was repulsed on Enborne Heath. A second charge met with the same result, Rupert being driven back on to the main Royalist infantry. However, the third charge was successful: Stapleton was routed and Rupert's horse pursued him, only to be shot down in the narrow lanes. By this time the carnage on both sides was immense.

Skippon now stabilised the centre by bringing forward the Trained Bands, and he also brought forward his guns to engage the Cavalier artillery which had been firing heavily at the Trained Bands. This led to probably the most intense artillery duel of the entire war. The Royalist foot was hotly engaged and the Roundheads certainly had the best of the battle there. Nonetheless, as they did not retreat the Royalists might have won the battle for the King now if they had shown any resolve, but their demeanour (according to accounts of the time) was spineless.

The northern part of the battle was never as intense as in the centre and south, and the only notable incident was when Vavasour's regiments drove back some Parliamentary cavalry and infantry attempting to ford the River Kennet.

At nightfall the battle died down. The Roundheads had had the best of the fight, although they were not looking forward to resuming the battle on the following day, but Charles's army was still unbroken and still barred the way to London. Rupert and Byron wanted to continue the battle, but the Royalists were running short of ammunition (an expected train from Oxford having not arrived), and there was the usual difference of opinion at their council of war as to whether to hold their ground or to withdraw. The King's opinions eventually overruled the rest, and over-cautious as ever and strongly supported by Lord Forth, his chief of staff, he withdrew into Newbury with the intention of returning to Oxford. His army had suffered heavy casualties and was short of powder, but why this decision was taken is not known, because it left Essex's route open. The King had given up the great advantage which his men had suffered so gallantly to achieve and maintain.

During the battle the Royalists had suffered heavily in senior commanders killed. Besides Lord Falkland, who had been Secretary of State and whose post was now taken over by Lord Digby (which was eventually to produce fatal results because of his great influence with the King), Lord Carnarvon and Lord Sunderland had also been killed. The total number of dead from both sides was probably about 3,500.

Essex was amazed at finding the field empty on the following morning, but gladly took advantage of his good luck and marched on to Reading. He was attacked en route by a party of Cavalier horse under Rupert near Aldermaston, which created considerable panic but few losses, and on 28 September he re-entered London to the cheers of the crowds. He had halted the tide of Royalist successes and put London itself farther than ever from the King's grasp.

MAP 18

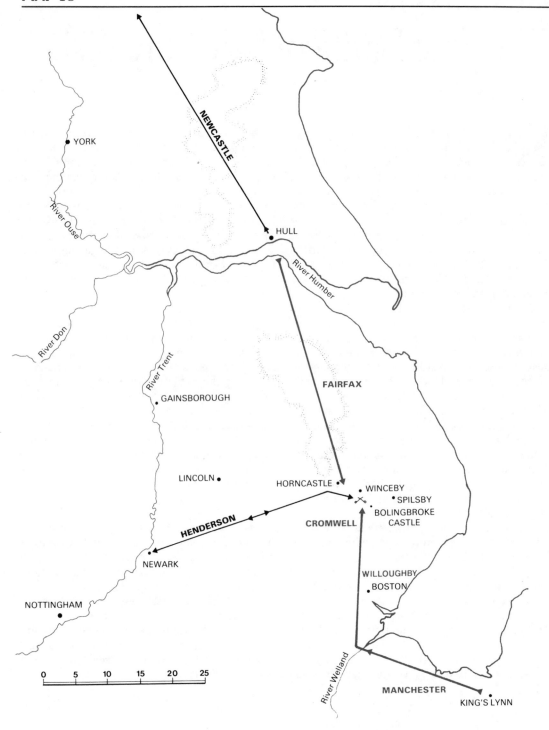

YORK

River Ouse

NEWCASTLE

HULL

River Humber

River Don

FAIRFAX

River Trent

GAINSBOROUGH

LINCOLN

HORNCASTLE

WINCEBY

SPILSBY

BOLINGBROKE
CASTLE

CROMWELL

HENDERSON

NEWARK

WILLOUGHBY

BOSTON

NOTTINGHAM

River Welland

MANCHESTER

KING'S LYNN

0   5   10   15   20   25

MAP 18

Actions at Winceby and Hull

September–8 December 1643

DURING the winter of 1643-44 much of the action centred on the northern theatre of operations, although there were some significant Royalist successes in the south. In Ireland a peace, or at least a cessation of hostilities, had been arranged, which allowed English troops fighting the Irish rebels to be brought back to swell the Royalist army.

In September Newcastle, who had been created a Marquess after the battle of Adwalton Moor, was investing Hull. For the Roundheads, Manchester was investing King's Lynn; Cromwell with the cavalry of the Eastern Association of counties, and Sir Thomas Fairfax, who had escaped from Hull with the cavalry there to relieve the town of the burden of feeding them and had joined Cromwell, were besieging Bolingbroke castle a few miles from Spilsby in Lincolnshire; and Lord Willoughby was besieging Boston.

On 16 September King's Lynn surrendered, and Manchester marched north to join Fairfax and Cromwell, who had meanwhile delivered some much-needed supplies to the beleaguered garrison of Hull. On 10 October the Royalist Sir John Henderson, who was governor of Newark, arrived with a strong body of horse to relieve the garrison of Bolingbroke; he encountered Fairfax with a small party of horse near Horncastle and drove him off. Cromwell would have preferred not to fight a battle as his horse were in poor condition, but now had no option but to attack Henderson. They met at the hamlet of Winceby, five miles east of Horncastle on the road to Spilsby, and Cromwell charged him. Fairfax now re-entered the fray with fresh horse, charged Henderson again, and routed him, causing so much damage that only a few of the Royalist cavalry managed to return to Newark, leaving Bolingbroke still under siege.

Newcastle, who was a good soldier but had little support because the main Cavalier armies were in the south and west, was having problems at Hull. Much of his army consisted of unwilling conscripts who would much rather have been back on their farms in Yorkshire, and about half of them deserted and returned home. Then on 11 October the garrison at Hull sallied out and attacked him, capturing some of his forts and cannon, and so weak was Newcastle now that he had to raise the siege the following day.

Eight days later the Roundheads captured Lincoln. Newcastle's threat to London had evaporated, and there were even fears of an invasion from Scotland in support of Parliament. In order to protect the north the King now formed a weak new army under Lord Byron (Sir John having been raised to the peerage after the battle of Newbury), which set off for Cheshire. On 8 December 1643 Pym, who had master-minded the Parliamentary break with the King, died and was buried in Henry VII's chapel in Westminster Abbey.

MAP 19

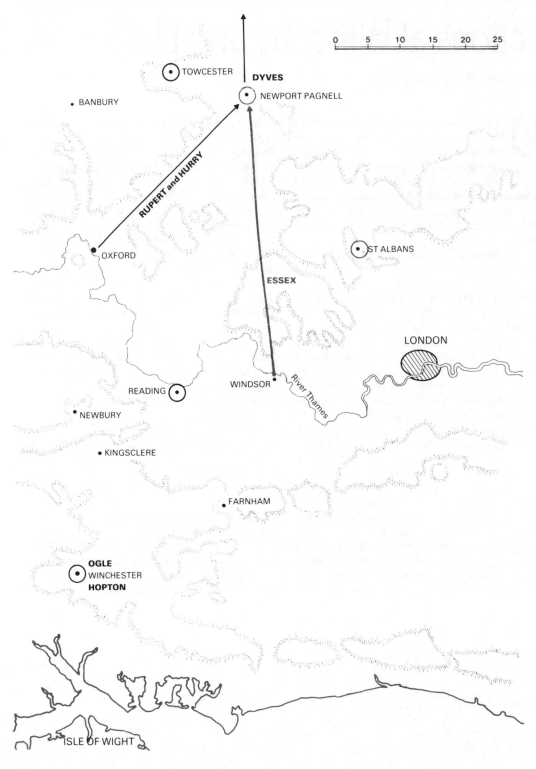

0   5   10   15   20   25

TOWCESTER

DYVES

BANBURY

⊙ NEWPORT PAGNELL

RUPERT and HURRY

⊙ ST ALBANS

OXFORD

ESSEX

LONDON

READING ⊙

WINDSOR   River Thames

NEWBURY

KINGSCLERE

FARNHAM

OGLE
WINCHESTER
HOPTON

ISLE OF WIGHT

MAP 19

Minor Actions in the South and West

28 September–November 1643

THE Trained Bands, being composed largely of shopkeepers in London, were anxious to return to their businesses when they reached London with Essex after the battle of Newbury, and their departure so weakened the army that Essex had to abandon Reading and fall back on Windsor. The Royalists reoccupied Reading and the King installed Sir Jacob Astley as governor.

On 6 October Prince Maurice, once more back in Devon, captured Dartmouth, one of the few remaining Parliamentary strongholds in the southwest, in a surprise attack. With the town he siezed 40 ships belonging to London merchants which were in port, so Sir John Pennington now had more ships at sea than the Roundheads under the Earl of Warwick and was able to blockade Plymouth while Maurice besieged it by land (see Map 14). Warwick was alarmed at the situation although Parliament obviously did not seem to share his views, because it provided few men and little money to keep the fleet afloat. Nevertheless, it appointed Warwick as Lord High Admiral in place of the Earl of Northumberland on 7 December.

In London the City magnates and merchants began to appreciate Essex's weakness without the Trained Bands, and such was the support for Parliament among Londoners that a number of regiments volunteered to re-form and help Essex regain Reading. Essex planned to march on Reading on 18 October, but by then other more pressing matters had occurred which caused this expedition to be abandoned, at least temporarily.

On 15 October Rupert, with Hurry, had set out on an expedition to the Midlands and seized Newport Pagnall, establishing a garrison there under Sir Lewis Dyves before setting off to plunder Northamptonshire and Bedfordshire. This was a significant loss to Parliament because the town commanded the communications between London and the north, and it also gave the Royalists a platform from which to advance into East Anglia. Essex marched his new Trained Bands thither instead of to Reading, and Dyves, perhaps misunderstanding an order but perhaps also sensing danger from the approaching storm, abandoned the town, which Essex then entered and fortified. Essex also fortified St Albans, and the Royalists fortified Towcester.

In November Lord Hopton, although he really believed that it would be better to move southwestwards again and capture the few Roundhead fortresses in Wiltshire and Dorset, had been ordered into Hampshire with a small army. Unfortunately this no longer included his Cornishmen, who had gone home, and he had to replace them with raw levies and some unreliable regiments which had returned from Ireland. Sir William Ogle had captured Winchester for the Royalists in a surprise attack, and Hopton occupied the city and made it his base.

MAP 20

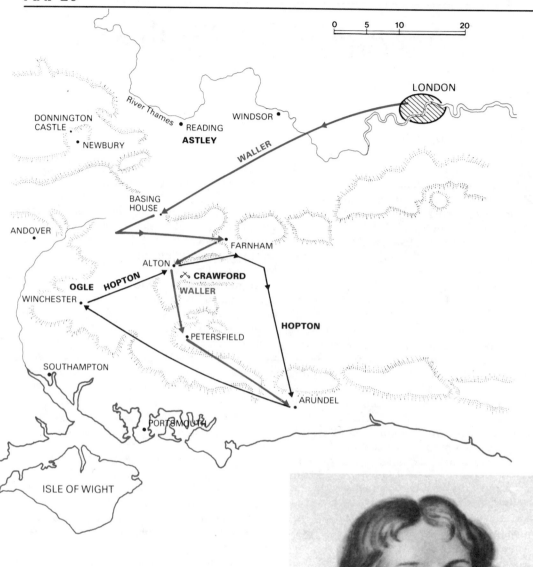

0   5   10   20

LONDON

River Thames

WINDSOR

DONNINGTON CASTLE

READING

ASTLEY

NEWBURY

WALLER

BASING HOUSE

ANDOVER

FARNHAM

ALTON

✕ **CRAWFORD**

OGLE   **HOPTON**

WALLER

WINCHESTER

HOPTON

PETERSFIELD

SOUTHAMPTON

ARUNDEL

PORTSMOUTH

ISLE OF WIGHT

Sir Philip Stapleton (1603-1647)

A gallant gentleman, thin and sickly but tenacious, he was one of the best Roundhead cavalry commanders. He was a landowner, an MP and leader of the Presbyterians in Parliament, being deprived of his command by the Self Denying Ordinance. In 1647 he was impeached, but escaped and died in Calais.

MAP 20

The Actions of Basing House and Arundel

November 1643–6 January 1644

WALLER was now commander of the southeastern Parliamentary forces and set out to capture Basing House, near Basingstoke. This was a fortified mansion of the Marquess of Winchester, one of the King's Catholic supporters, and had been occupied by the Royalists to command the southern road from London to Salisbury and the southwest, in the same way as Donnington castle at Newbury was now garrisoned to command the northern route. Waller's first attack was frustrated by extremely bad weather, and his second by a London regiment refusing to obey orders. A third attack two days later was foiled by the desertion of many of the Trained Bands who decided that they had had enough and anyway wanted to return to London.

Instead of capturing Basing House, Waller decided to advance to Winchester. When he heard of Hopton's arrival there, and with memories of the troops he had fought at Lansdown and Roundway Down (not knowing that they were no longer with Hopton), he immediately withdrew to Farnham. Hopton followed him up with his whole force and garrisoned Alton with a detachment under Lord Crawford.

At this point Hopton was brought news, probably false, of strong support in Kent and Sussex, which suggested that a march to that area would secure the southeast for the King. Charles was overjoyed by this news, and although he had previously decided that Hopton should stay on the defensive to keep Waller committed, now ordered him to march into Sussex. Hopton set off to Farnham, but, finding that Waller had fortified the town strongly, bypassed it and moved on to Arundel. This he captured, including the castle, on 9 December.

Hopton was now overstretched and in considerable danger, with Waller, reinforced by two more regiments from London, on his flank. On 13 December Waller surprised the detachment at Alton, as Hopton had warned Crawford might happen and about which he had told him to be on his guard. Although Crawford defended strongly during a fierce battle his few infantry were forced to surrender and he only managed to escape with some of his horse. Many prisoners were taken and — as had happened on a number of previous occasions — many of them joined the Roundheads. For some unknown reason the London regiment which had refused to fight at Basing House fought bravely here.

Hopton, in his weakend condition, now abandoned Petersfield. It was occupied at once by the Parliamentarians, and Waller, having marched to Arundel, recaptured the town and castle on 6 January 1644. Hopton was forced to retire to Winchester, in the event safely but with some difficulty because Petersfield lay on his route.

MAP 21

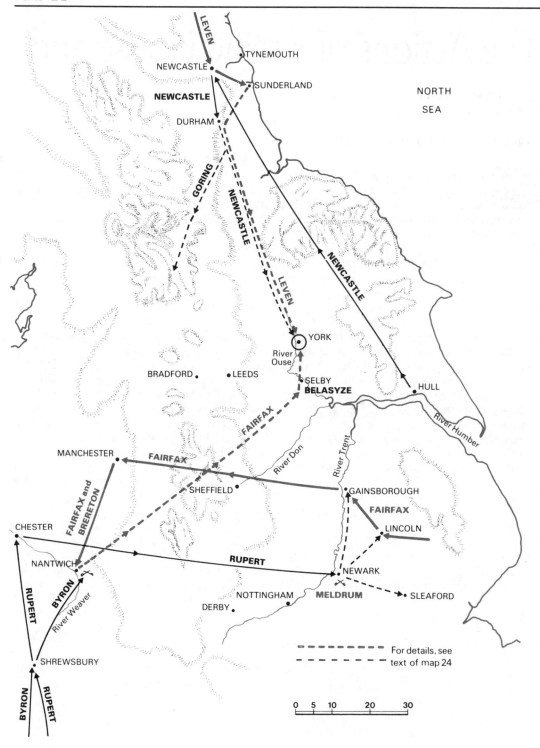

For details, see
text of map 24

0 5 10   20   30

MAP 21

Actions at Nantwich and Newark

13 December 1643–20 April 1644

ON 13 December Lord Byron had arrived in Cheshire and laid siege to Nantwich, the last Roundhead stronghold in the county; but with Newcastle having raised the siege of Hull in October the Roundheads now had greater freedom of movement. Fairfax took Gainsborough again, moved to Manchester where he was joined by Sir William Brereton, and set off to relieve Nantwich. On 25 January 1644 he attacked Byron, whose army was divided by the River Weaver which had suddenly come into flood. Two of Byron's regiments brought over from Ireland broke and fled; the garrison of the town, seeing the situation, came out to help, and the Royalists were utterly defeated. Byron managed to escape with his cavalry, but more than half of the remainder of his army was taken prisoner, many of them joining the Parliamentary army. Among them was Colonel Monck, who many years later was to gain fame at the time of Charles II's restoration and raise the present-day Coldstream Guards.

On 15 January a Scottish army of over 20,000 men under Lord Leven invaded England to support the Parliamentary cause, and the Royalists in Northumberland retreated into the town of Newcastle, where the Marquess of Newcastle was also in danger of being attacked by Fairfax from the south and wrote urgently to the King for immediate help. Leven halted for a while and then carried on southwards, driving Newcastle before him. The Scots occupied Sunderland, and Lord Newcastle retreated to Durham.

At Durham, Newcastle was joined on 15 March by the Earl of Montrose. He was to become a most important figure for the rest of the war and had for long been urging the King to let him have a free hand against the Covenanters in Scotland, and did so again when the Covenanter army invaded England. Montrose asked Newcastle for troops, but the latter was so weak that he could not oblige beyond a few cavalry and called out the militia in the northwest to help. Montrose set off on his first expedition to Scotland.

Meanwhile Prince Rupert was on his way north from Oxford, reaching Shrewsbury on 21 February and then Chester, where he tried unsuccessfully to raise an army. Sir John Meldrum invested Newark, always a thorn in the side of the Roundheads, on 6 March, and Rupert was ordered to march to relieve the town, having still only a weak force at his command but collecting recruits from Royalist garrisons on the way. On 21 March he reached the outskirts of Newark with part of his force and pinned Meldrum down with it, to stop him withdrawing, until the rest of his army arrived.

After a bitter and bloody struggle Meldrum was defeated and surrendered the town, which provided a welcome cache of arms and ammunition for Rupert. The Royalists now gained control of the western part of Lincolnshire again and recaptured Gainsborough, Lincoln and Sleaford, but Rupert's army was too attenuated by then, after leaving garrisons, to advance to Hull or into the eastern counties. He was even too weak to leave garrisons in the towns which he had taken, as he had to return men to the other garrisons from which he had gathered them on his march. It was a hollow victory and did little to advance the Royalist cause.

MAP 22

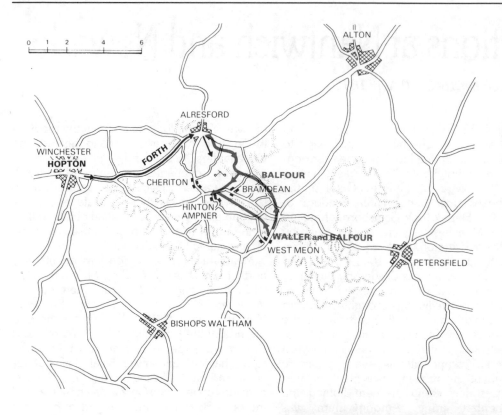

Alexander Leslie, Earl of Leven (c1580-1661)

Illegitimate, he entered Swedish service and fought in the 30 Years War. He returned to join the Roundheads and was nominal commander of the Scottish army which entered England. He later joined David Leslie to oppose Cromwell, was imprisoned and later released. He enjoyed great devotion from his troops.
National Galleries of Scotland

MAP 22

Minor Actions in the South

February–27 March 1644

AT THE end of February Parliament planned an attack on Oxford by Essex and an expedition to reconquer the west and southwest by Waller. The latter part of the plan was over-ambitious (a common fault from which both sides in the conflict suffered), but it was desirable mainly bacause every square mile of ground or town captured gained the Parliamentarians more resources and income and denied the same to the enemy.

Parliament also planned an action which it no doubt considered justified but which, if carried out by the Royalists, it would have condemned as treachery. This, of course, it was, because the Parliamentarians believed that Lord Charles Paulet who held Basing House could be persuaded to defect and hand the stronghold over to them. At the council of war which decided on this endeavour was Sir Bevil Grenville's brother, Sir Richard, an experienced though unreliable soldier who had been captured by the Roundheads on landing from Ireland and who, promising to support their cause, had been made a Lieutenant General of Horse. But it was Grenville himself who defected and fled from London to Oxford, taking with him the Parliamentary plan and the news of Paulet's possible treachery. Paulet was arrested, courtmartialled and sentenced to death, but was then pardoned by the King as a kinsman of one of his most loyal supporters, the Marquess of Winchester. Such were the wheelings and dealings of both sides during the war.

In March Hopton was still at Winchester, and Waller, having been joined by a large body of horse under Balfour, was at West Meon, guarding the road to Petersfield before advancing on the city. Hopton was joined by a force under Lord Forth, who was nominally Commander-in-Chief. Although Forth was a brave man and a fine tactician, he thought himself to be incompetent through age and asked Hopton to remain in command. As Forth was fond of the bottle and suffered from gout, and was also deaf, this was used as a good excuse for him not taking over command!

Nevertheless, Forth, on 27 March, advanced quickly to Alresford and occupied the town before Waller — who had belatedly realised its strategic importance — could get there, although a body of horse under Balfour was only just beaten to it. Waller, with an army of 10,000 men (of which over a third was cavalry), halted south of the town between Cheriton and Bramdean at Hinton Ampner; Forth established his army, outnumbered by two to one, on a hill between Alresford and Cheriton and sent a detachment to guard the hill in front on which was Cheriton Wood. Waller may have thought of retiring but more probably employed a stratagem used by Wellington in the Peninsula many years later. During the night he withdrew some wagons with much noise, which convinced the Royalists that he was retreating, thus achieving his objective of putting them off their guard.

MAP 23

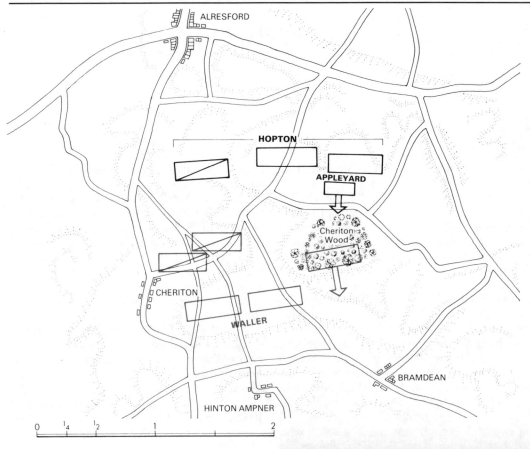

**Patrick Ruthven, Earl of Forth and Brentford
(c1573-1651)**

Born in Scotland, he served in the Swedish army for many years. He was an honourable man, brave, resourceful and skilled in the art of war. In 1642 he joined the King, was made Commander-in-Chief although he was then 70 years old, and was created Earl of Forth. Age, deafness and wounds eventually had their effect and he was replaced by Prince Rupert. He went to Scotland with Charles II in 1650, then retired to his estates and died in Dundee. *National Galleries of Scotland*

MAP 23

The Battle of Cheriton

29 March 1644

AT DAWN on the morning of 29 March, in a thick mist, Waller threw a strong force into Cheriton Wood. The Royalist detachment, finding itself outflanked and outnumbered, withdrew. Waller, in deploying his army, also went against the normal practice of using cavalry on the wings of the infantry and established his horse on a common to the west of the ridge and in front of the foot. (It must be said here that contemporary accounts of the battle are confusing and the exact location of the troops taking part is difficult to discover.)

Hopton, having arrived on the scene, ordered a small body under Colonel Appleyard to clear the wood, and although it was defended gallantly he eventually drove the enemy headlong from it. Hopton now wanted to make a major assault with horse and foot, but Forth, ever cautious, persuaded him not to do so, believing that Waller must now retreat and in so doing lay himself open to a disaster which could open the way southeast to the King. However, a regiment of horse under Sir Henry Bard did attack, against orders, and was destroyed by the Roundhead cavalry on the common. Other regiments followed and they were overpowered one by one before they could deploy as they came from a lane on to the open ground. Waller's dispositions had justified themselves, but this was an example of a defeat caused primarily by disobedience of orders.

Nevertheless, for some hours the battle raged furiously, but with surprisingly few casualties, both sides showing great gallantry and determination. Eventually Hazlerigg's very experienced horse, found a gap in the Royalist defences and, pushing through it, routed the Royalist infantry. This action virtually decided the day, although Hopton managed to gather a body of horse around him and stem the Roundhead advance until the remainder of the army had been able to carry out an orderly withdrawal to the position which it had held at the beginning of the day. Among the dead in the battle was Sir John Smith, who had rescued the Royal Standard at Edgehill.

Hopton and Forth now burnt Alresford and retreated first to Basing House and thence to Oxford. The battle, the first major decisive Parliamentary victory, was a disaster for Charles who thereby lost any chance he may have had of advancing into the southeast.

Waller now occupied Winchester on 30 March, also took Andover, Salisbury and Christchurch, and threatened to advance into Dorset. But when his London regiments insisted on returning home he was forced to withdraw to his old fortified base at Farnham. He was back to where he started, but the Royalist cause had suffered a blow from which it never recovered.

Parliament was now making gains in all areas of the country.

MAP 24

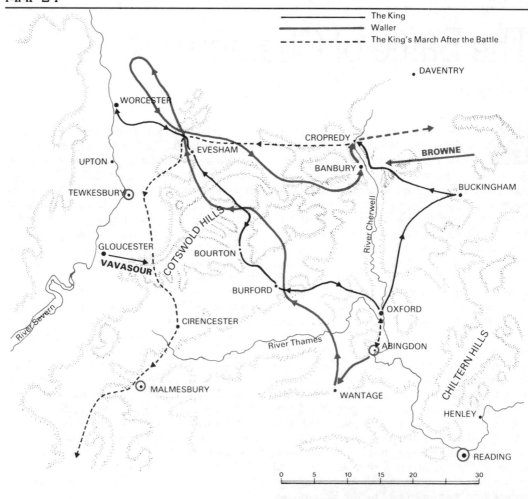

The King
Waller
The King's March After the Battle

DAVENTRY

WORCESTER

CROPREDY

EVESHAM

BROWNE

UPTON

BANBURY

BUCKINGHAM

TEWKESBURY

River Cherwell

COTSWOLD HILLS

GLOUCESTER

BOURTON

VAVASOUR

BURFORD

OXFORD

CIRENCESTER

River Thames

ABINGDON

CHILTERN HILLS

River Severn

MALMESBURY

WANTAGE

HENLEY

READING

0   5   10   15   20   30

Sir Thomas Fairfax (1612-1671)

A man of culture and learning, born in Yorkshire, he was
the best of the Parliamentary commanders. He went to
serve abroad at 17, later served the King in the Scottish
wars, but on the outbreak of the Civil War joined the
Parliamentary army. Distinguishing himself in the early
fighting as a cavalry leader, he became Commander-in-
Chief of the New Model Army on its formation. He
became 3rd Baron Fairfax on his father's death in 1648,
had little sympathy for the extreme Puritans, was not a
regicide and later helped to bring about the Restoration.
He died at Nun Appleton.

MAP 24

Actions before Cropredy Bridge

11 April–June 1644

ON 11 APRIL Lord Belasyze had been defeated when Selby in Yorkshire was stormed by Sir Thomas Fairfax, and he and thousands of prisoners were captured. (See Map 21.) Newcastle, worried about the safety of York, marched his infantry there to strengthen the garrison, sending his cavalry off with Goring to join Prince Rupert. He arrived just in time on 20 April, since Lord Fairfax and the Earl of Leven had joined forces, intending to besiege the city — although not very closely at first — only a few days later with some 22,000 men. Charles was getting worried too, but made a grave mistake by recalling Sir William Vavasour from the siege of Gloucester to Oxford, thus allowing the Roundheads to resupply the city with ammunition, which at this time was almost expended.

Rupert too was recalled to Oxford, but left his army in the north to help Lord Newcastle because he believed that York must be relieved as soon as possible. Charles became more and more despondent and irresolute, in spite of Rupert's efforts to encourage him and to force decisions from him, and his policy now seemed to be based on defence rather than offence. Towns in the west were rebelling against the Royalists, some of them as the result of Prince Maurice's harsh actions against them: Reading was abandoned on 18 May and Abingdon a week later. On 24 May Malmesbury surrendered to the Roundheads and Waller, having occupied Abingdon, marched to Wantage to attempt to cut the King off from the southwest.

At last Charles was goaded into some action as it became clear that if he were to shut himself up in Oxford the city would soon be starved out and he would be captured. On 3 June he made a feint attack on Abingdon which drew Waller back to its defence, and then set out from the city during the night, with some 7,000 men, to Burford and Bourton-on-the-Water, and thence to Evesham. There he learned that Tewkesbury had also surrendered, and that whilst a small army was advancing south from Staffordshire, Essex and Waller were on his track. The King was too weak to fight a battle against the combined Roundhead armies and marched on to Worcester.

Now dissent arose in the Parliamentary councils about the best action to be taken. Instead of doing the obvious thing and the joint armies marching after the King and bringing him to battle, it was decided that Essex, having a widely recruited army, should march to the southwest and try to raise the siege of Lyme, while Waller, with his army composed mostly of London regiments who refused to move far from home, should continue his chase of the King. Essex in fact took his whole army with him, informing Parliament that Waller was unfit to recapture the southwest, and that after taking the King he should return to the siege of Oxford. Animosity between Essex and Waller was still strong, and it is difficult to see why Essex needed 10,000 men to raise a siege, and could not have left some of his army behind.

MAP 25

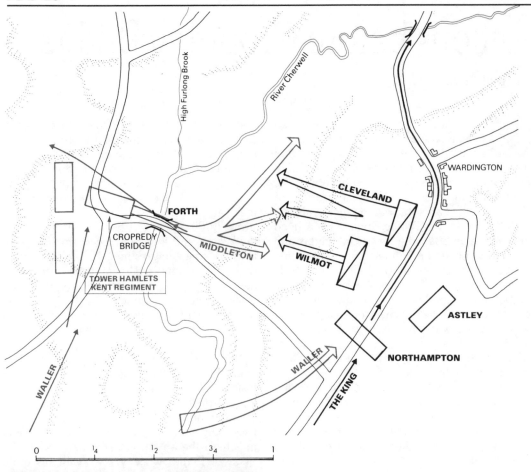

River Cherwell

High Furlong Brook

WARDINGTON

CLEVELAND

FORTH

CROPREDY
BRIDGE

MIDDLETON

WILMOT

TOWER HAMLETS
KENT REGIMENT

ASTLEY

NORTHAMPTON

WALLER

WALLER

THE KING

0   ¼   ½   ¾   1

Sir Jacob (Lord) Astley (1579-1652)

Born in Norfolk, he served abroad for a long period. He joined the King at Nottingham in 1642, and gained fame for his prayer before Edgehill: 'Lord, thou knowest how busy I must be this day. If I forget thee, do not thou forget me.' He retired after the war and died at Maidstone. *In a private collection*

MAP 25

The Battle of Cropredy Bridge

23 May–29 June 1644

SINCE the middle of April Prince Maurice had been besieging Lyme, but in spite of many strong attacks the town maintained a determined resistance, and on 23 May Warwick arrived off the port with much-needed supplies. As Essex neared Lyme on 15 June, Maurice perforce raised the siege and the Roundheads occupied the town, and Weymouth, before pushing on westwards.

Charles, realising that the Parliamentary armies had split, returned to Oxford (which was no longer under siege) to collect more troops and then to attack Waller. Having added a further 10,000 men to his army he turned north again and on 21 June he was at Buckingham with Waller close on his heels. Major General Browne was now sent from London to help Waller, but his army was small and untrained and Waller waited so that he could join him. Together they took up a strong position near Banbury.

The Royalists turned towards Daventry to entice Waller into the open again — in which they succeeded Browne being left at Banbury — and the two armies marched northwards side by side and in view of each other, but about two miles apart separated by the River Cherwell. On 29 June the Earl of Brentford, as Forth had now become, seized Cropredy Bridge, a few miles north of Banbury with a small detachment. Charles now pressed on to join him with his vanguard, unfortunately not informing the main body of what he was doing nor of his increase in pace, so that a large gap opened in his army. Waller saw his chance and attacked the outpost at Cropredy Bridge, capturing it, and the main Royalist army came hurrying to the aid of the vanguard and the detachment.

The Earl of Cleveland, commanding a brigade of Royalist cavalry, charged the Roundheads at the bridge, and Middleton, the Parliamentary commander of the horse, was routed after a desperate battle. Lord Wilmot joined Cleveland and another charge captured all the Roundhead artillery. Charles was thus in a strong position, even though Browne was now at Buckingham in his rear; but instead of attacking Waller — albeit he was in a good position on a ridge but nevertheless without much cavalry and with no guns — he tried, obviously without any success, to make terms with him. Once again he had thrown away a glorious opportunity of destroying Waller's army. No general, and the King was no general anyway, could hope to make as many mistakes as Charles had done and still have any hope of winning the war.

MAP 26

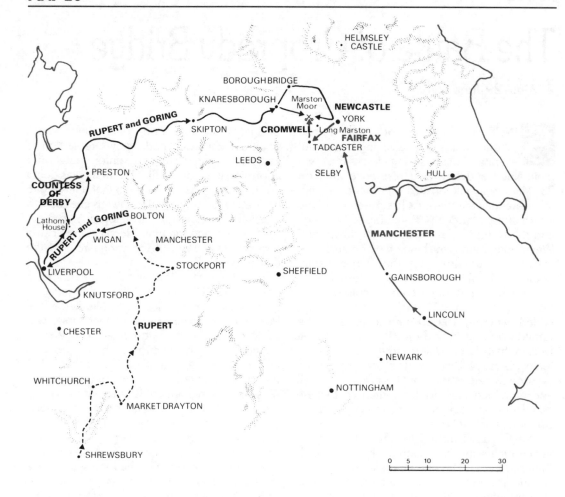

MAP 26

The Approach to Marston Moor

April–1 July 1644

ON 6 MAY the Earl of Manchester stormed and captured Lincoln, then Gainsborough, and at the beginning of June was able to march his army of about 6,000 men to join the besiegers of York. During April and May Lathom House, the home of the Earl of Derby between Liverpool and Preston, had been besieged by the Roundheads, but its defender, the Countess, had defied all efforts to capture it. On 16 May Rupert set out from Shrewsbury, not directly to York to relieve the siege, but to Lancashire to raise the siege of Lathom House and thereby gather more recruits.

He seized Stockport on 25 May, bypassed the Parliamentary garrison town of Manchester and on the 28th stormed Bolton, defeating there the besiegers of Lathom House who had withdrawn at his approach. The Roundheads suffered very heavy casualties and the town was sacked. On 1 June Goring joined Rupert with the strong body of horse detached from Newcastle's army when it withdrew to York. Rupert carried on through Wigan, recruits now pouring in, and assaulted Liverpool. Initially the attack was repulsed but the defenders took to the ships and sailed away during the night: the town fell on 11 June, the remaining Roundheads being butchered.

The Parliamentary generals, Manchester and Fairfax, refused to abandon the siege of York although Parliament was alarmed at the situation, but offered to put out cavalry patrols under Cromwell to guard the approaches to the city, and only to give up the siege if Rupert approached too close. Newcastle now offered to surrender York, partly to save the city from damage but also because he had only provisions for a few more days; but because he wanted to march out with the honours of war and the Roundheads wanted to defeat him in detail, this was refused. On 16 June a mine was exploded under St Mary's Tower, originally part of a monastery and now one of the key defences of the city. It went off prematurely and the follow-up attack by the Roundheads was badly mauled by the defenders of the city and suffered heavy casualties.

By the 30th Rupert had crossed the Pennines and was at Knaresborough, and the besiegers were in danger — as Sir John Meldrum had been at Newark and as Charles had anticipated being at Gloucester — of being caught between the defenders of the city and an avenging army. On 1 July therefore they marched out to Long Marston on the road to Knaresborough to defend the route to the city. Rupert left a cavalry screen on Marston Moor as a decoy and with the rest of his army swept round through Boroughbridge and approached York from the north instead of from the west, and the city was relieved. The Roundhead army fell back towards Tadcaster, believing that Rupert would now move south towards Newark, but Cromwell with his horse was still on Marston Moor, and when he saw Rupert's cavalry screen in front of him being reinforced he summoned the Roundhead army back.

MAP 27

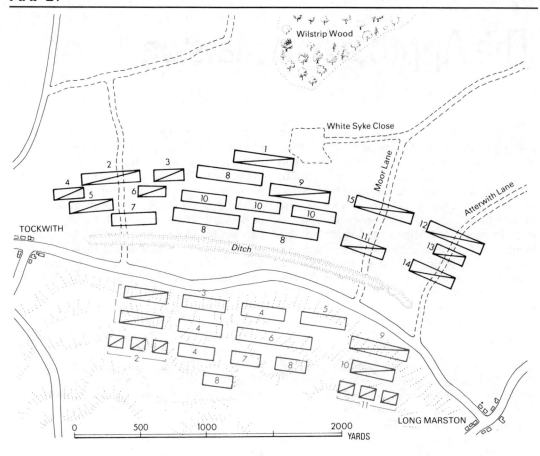

Wilstrip Wood

White Syke Close

Moor Lane

Atterwith Lane

1

2   3

4   8   9

5   6

7   10   10   15

10   12

8   13

8   14

TOCKWITH

Ditch

3

1   4   5

4

2   4   6   9

7   8

8   10

11

LONG MARSTON

0   500   1000   2000
YARDS

1 Reserve Horse (Prince Rupert)

2 Molyneux
3 Prince Rupert   } Byron
4 Tuke
5 Byron

6 Trevor
7 Napier
8 Eythin
9 Blakiston
10 Newcastle's Whitecoats

11 Goring
12 Dacre
13 Carnaby   } Goring
14 Langdale (Lucas)
15 Lucas

1 Cromwell
2 Sir David Leslie's Scots Horse   } Cromwell

3 Crawford
4 Lord Fairfax
5 Baillie
6 Lumsden's Scots Foot
7 Scots Foot
8 Manchester

9 Sir Thomas Fairfax
10 Lambert   } Fairfax
11 Eglington's Scots Horse

MAP 27

The Battle of Marston Moor (1)

2 July 1644

INSTEAD of going to York himself to discuss battle plans with Newcastle, Rupert unfortunately sent Lord Goring to order Newcastle to join Rupert on Marston Moor. Goring, not being the most tactful of men, clearly upset Newcastle who refused to co-operate. Newcastle proposed waiting before a battle was joined, in the hope that reinforcements might arrive from Montrose, but Rupert was never one to display caution, even though his troops were exhausted after a long march.

Rupert also had a letter from the King entreating him to relieve York and, as be believed (although the wording is ambiguous and may have been 'doctored' by Digby), destroy the Roundhead army in the north if he was to continue the fight. Newcastle, still loath to move and to come under Rupert's command, nevertheless now agreed to come out of York to help Rupert. By the afternoon of 2 July both armies were deploying, the Roundheads having returned rapidly and having considerable superiority in numbers, probably about 27,000 to 18,000.

The Roundheads were positioned on the south of the battlefield on the slopes and summit of a long ridge. On the right was Sir Thomas Fairfax's horse and some Scottish cavalry, with Manchester's regiment; in the centre were Baillie and Lumsden with the infantry of Leven's army; on the left was Manchester and his army (with Crawford commanding the infantry) and Lord Fairfax; and Cromwell and Sir David Leslie's Scottish horse were on the flank.

On the Royalist side, to the north and on the Moor itself, Goring's horse was on the left opposite Fairfax, and Lord Byron's horse was on the right; Lord Eythin, Newcastle's Chief of Staff, was in the centre, later to be joined by Newcastle himself; while Prince Rupert, the commander for the battle, was in the rear with a small reserve of horse. The two armies were less than 400yd apart, with only a ditch and the Tockwith-Long Marston road, then a narrow rutted lane, between them. Lord Eythin, a veteran of the European wars but a poor commander, had a chip on his shoulder concerning Rupert relating to some incidents many years before. He disapproved and was very rude to Rupert about his dispositions, which he thought were all against current practice though apparently sensible on paper.

Prince Rupert had been all for attacking straight away, while the Roundheads were still moving up and deploying and therefore at a disadvantage, but Eythin had persuaded him that it was too late in the day to start a battle, particularly after it had been raining. The Parliamentarians obviously disagreed with Eythin's theory on late-starting battles and did not have his restraining influence on their actions, because around 7 o'clock in the evening, with another storm brewing and the Royalists clearly having stood down to have their supper, Leven seized his opportunity, saying that according to legend a summer's night was as long as a winter's day, and suddenly attacked. Rupert had no defensive position to fall back on even if he had wished and had to fight on his chosen ground. He immediately attacked Cromwell's horse with Byron's regiments and his own reserve. At first he was successful, and a furious battle raged to and fro, but eventually Cromwell, and Leslie from the flank, pushed him back and sent his erstwhile undefeated horse flying out of the battle.

MAP 28

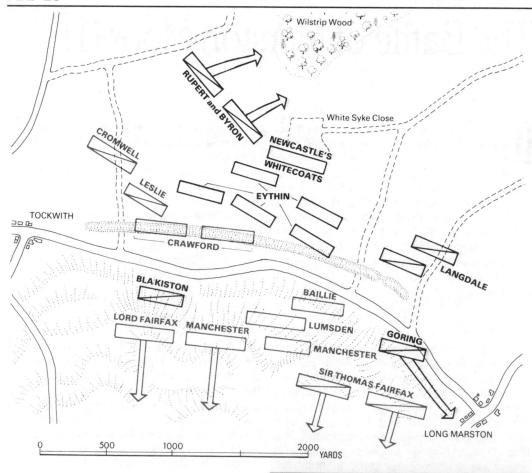

- Wilstrip Wood
- RUPERT and BYRON
- White Syke Close
- CROMWELL
- NEWCASTLE'S
- WHITECOATS
- LESLIE
- EYTHIN
- TOCKWITH
- CRAWFORD
- LANGDALE
- BLAKISTON
- BAILLIE
- LORD FAIRFAX
- MANCHESTER
- LUMSDEN
- GORING
- MANCHESTER
- SIR THOMAS FAIRFAX
- LONG MARSTON

0   500   1000   2000
YARDS

George, Lord Goring (1608-1657)

Goring was a complex character: he was a brilliant cavalry leader, bold, courageous and decisive, but was extremely ambitious, dissolute and a libertine. He joined the Dutch service and was lamed, returned to England as Governor of Portsmouth, and although Parliament thought that he supported them joined the Royalists. He succeeded Lord Wilmot as General of Horse, but after his defeat at Langport he retired to France. He joined the Spanish service and died in Madrid.

MAP 28

The Battle of Marston Moor (2)

2 July 1644

IT WAS at this point that Newcastle's regiment of Whitecoats, so called from their undyed woollen uniforms, arrived on the scene from York. In the centre the Roundheads under Crawford crossed the ditch at a point where it had been partially filled in and attacked the flank of Eythin's infantry, left unguarded by the cavalry battle. Although pushed back the Royalists did not break, and the battle raged there too in the gathering darkness. Blakiston's horse giving the Scots a hard time.

On the right the Roundheads were in trouble. The going there was difficult because the moor was covered with furze: Lord Fairfax's infantry was slowed down and the attack of Sir Thomas Fairfax's horse had to follow the narrow Moor Lane which was defended by Royalist musketeers and dragoons. Sir Thomas charged Goring's brigade of horse but after a long and fierce battle his main body was routed and the cavalry fell back on the infantry, scattering them. Most of Goring's horse followed in pursuit, giving rise to stories of a Royalist victory with much rejoicing, but then, instead of turning and attacking the remaining Roundhead foot, they stopped to plunder the baggage train. The horse that were left, mainly Blakiston's, joined with the Cavalier foot in assaulting Lumsden's Scottish infantry in the Roundhead centre, and although Leven and Lord Fairfax fled, Baillie stayed in the field; Manchester, who had also left, returned after a short absence.

All was now total confusion with both armies mixed up and locked in mortal combat, units often facing in quite a different direction to the one in which they had started the battle. The Royalist attacks were repulsed, although with heavy casualties, and the desperate struggle in the centre could not last long unless help came to the Roundheads there. But help was at hand, from Crawford's infantry which had as yet been little engaged. He supported Baillie and attacked towards the east, meeting Goring's horse returning from its plundering. In the narrow lanes with furze on all sides the Cavaliers now could not deploy and they were thrown back in confusion, to disaster.

In the centre of the Royalist line, Leslie's horse had now attacked Newcastle's regiment of Whitecoats, and driven back Rupert's horse; Rupert himself had to take cover in a beanfield and thus was unable to control the battle. The Whitecoats were fine soldiers and, having withdrawn to a stronger position at White Syke Close, held their ground; they died almost to a man where they stood because they would not surrender. Fairfax by now had assembled some of the horse, and riding round the Royalist rear attacked the infantry from behind. When Cromwell's horse came up to help Crawford and Baillie, resistance was soon over and the Roundheads had won a resounding victory. The Royalist army had lost over 4,000 killed and had ceased to exist as an organised fighting force. It has been said that the Royalists lost the battle more through their mistakes and blunders than through the expertise of the enemy.

The General Situation after Marston Moor

After the battle of Marston Moor, Newcastle could not accept the disgrace of defeat and fled with Eythin to Scarborough where they took ship for the Continent and exile, realising that all was lost. Rupert however, made of sterner stuff, gathered the remaining horse and rode to York, but without a relieving army in the field the city was untenable. Next morning Rupert set off back to Lancashire in the hope of gaining new recruits and retrieving the effects of the disaster with fresh victories, in spite of his orders from the King to save the city. But Rupert's reputation had been largely destroyed in the battle, he having left the field so early, and he could hope to gain little further support.

On 16 July the garrison of York, with nothing left to fight with or for, surrendered. Rupert's defeat had left the whole of the north (apart from a few isolated strongholds) in Parliamentary hands, and Fairfax and Manchester could now join Essex and Waller without danger to London.

Nonetheless, the battle of Marston Moor had created personal jealousies in the Parliamentary army. Writing after the battle, Cromwell had relegated Sir David Leslie's part in the battle to 'a few Scots in our rear', although they amounted to almost a third of the calvary force and had done sterling work, and he had given complete credit for the victory to himself — and to God. Cromwell was an intolerant man, aptly named 'Ironside' by Prince Rupert, and had little time for Manchester, Fairfax and Leven, who in his opinion did not give sufficient credit to God's blessing on their cause in the struggle.

The three generals had written to Parliament proposing that their major attention should now be given towards procuring peace, and in that proposal Cromwell was not included. Anyway, he did not agree with it, because he believed that anybody who did not share his religious fanaticism (ie the Royalists) had to be defeated soundly for their sins. The generals' armies now split up, Leven to cover the siege of Newcastle, Fairfax to subdue Yorkshire and Manchester to remain in readiness in East Anglia. None of them gave any thought to the likelihood of being needed in the south.

When Marston Moor was fought, Montrose was far away — in spite of Newcastle's hope of receiving reinforcements from him — still marching south from Durham and Sunderland. After the battle he returned to Scotland to try to raise the Royalist support there, but with little hope of success in such a strongly Presbyterian country. In the Highlands the main Parliamentary support came from the Marquess of Argyll and his Campbells in the west, with other Covenanter forces at Perth under Lord Elcho and at Aberdeen where Lord Balfour of Burleigh commanded a small army.

Montrose then learned, through intercepting a messenger, that the Earl of Antrim, now relieved from the intermittent fighting in Ireland, had managed to raise three regiments and bring them to Scotland to support the King, and was prepared to serve under Montrose. Montrose therefore raised his Standard at Blair Athol, and on 30 August, with his army consisting largely of Irishmen, set off towards Perth.

Meanwhile the King had managed to slip away after the battle at Cropredy Bridge, and Waller now realised that the Royalist army, composed of devoted long-service soldiers, was more easily manageable than the Roundhead one. The Parliamentarians relied largely on the Trained Bands and the county militia, none of whom were keen to stay away from home longer than necessary or for very long at all. Waller suggested that the Parliamentary army also should be rebuilt on the same lines with committed soldiers, recruited with no particular territorial allegiances. In fact he was proposing the New Model as it was to become.

Cromwell, the egoist, took the credit for the suggestion, but he was not its progenitor. After his junction with Browne before Cropredy Bridge and after the battle there, Waller's army, thinking that it had been relieved 'of duty or that it should have been, began to melt away, and Waller's proposal was accepted and put into effect by Parliament when it saw the effect of the current system on his army. On 20 July Waller reoccupied Abingdon, but this time with a small force of not more than 4,000 men, little more now being necessary.

Sir John (Lord) Byron (c1603-1652)

Although a successful Royalist commander, he was not a good tactician. He joined the King at York in 1642 and, after taking a leading part in early battles, successfully defended Chester until the end of the war. He was then exiled and died abroad.

Henry Wilmot, Earl of Rochester (1613-1658)

A fine horseman, he was said to be haughty, ambitious and a wit, but was always popular with his men. He joined the King in 1642 and was a successful commander, but he hated Prince Rupert. Dismissed for an alleged plot to depose the King and exiled, he returned with Charles II and accompanied him during his escape. He died at Sluys.

MAP 29

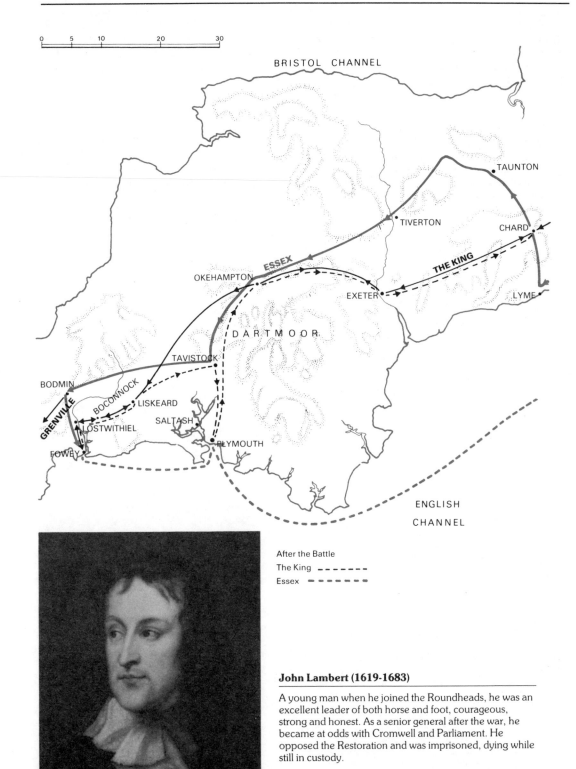

0   5   10   20   30

BRISTOL CHANNEL

TAUNTON

TIVERTON

CHARD

OKEHAMPTON   *ESSEX*

THE KING

EXETER

LYME

DARTMOOR

TAVISTOCK

BODMIN

BOCONNOCK   LISKEARD

GRENVILLE

SALTASH

LOSTWITHIEL

FOWEY

PLYMOUTH

ENGLISH
CHANNEL

After the Battle
The King ---------
Essex   ---------

John Lambert (1619-1683)

A young man when he joined the Roundheads, he was an
excellent leader of both horse and foot, courageous,
strong and honest. As a senior general after the war, he
became at odds with Cromwell and Parliament. He
opposed the Restoration and was imprisoned, dying while
still in custody.

MAP 29

The March to the Southwest

12 July–7 August 1644

WITH Waller more or less impotent, Essex's advance into the west became extremely hazardous. On 12 July Charles left Evesham (whence he had retired from Cropredy Bridge) for the southwest, and marched through Cirencester to Bath. There he heard of the disaster of Marston Moor. (See Map 24.) He was very bitter, not surprisingly, at the desertion of Newcastle and Eythin, and at Rupert's failure to carry out his orders to hold York, and it made him determined to follow Essex. However, he was unable to gather many recruits on the way because by now the populance was apparently becoming indifferent to both sides and to the conflict generally.

The Earl of Essex marched on westwards and relieved Lyme in the middle of June; then, having occupied Taunton early in July, he reached Tavistock and relieved Plymouth, realising by this time that he had a large Royalist army in his rear, since on 26 July Charles had reached Exeter and been joined by Prince Maurice. Nevertheless Essex marched into Cornwall, driving Sir Richard Grenville before him, and reached Bodmin while Grenville retired to Truro. The Cornishmen, being independent by nature, did not particularly relish an invasion of their county by either side, but they were solidly behind the King and he entered Liskeard on 2 August.

Essex marched to Lostwithiel and Fowey where he could keep in touch with the Roundhead fleet, hoping now either to be reinforced or, if necessary, for his army to be taken off by it. He called on Parliament for resupply by sea and for a diversion to be made by Waller to draw off the Cavaliers. The latter was impossible in Waller's weak condition, although it appears that Essex did not know this. Charles, ever hopeful, contacted Essex with offers of a peace treaty, but Essex, ever loyal, refused to consider such a thing without authority from Parliament.

It had been rumoured to the King that Lord Wilmot had suggested deposing Charles and placing the Prince of Wales on the throne: it is not clear who spread the rumour but jealousy was still rife in the army. Loyal as he was, it is probable that Wilmot (if he ever said such a thing) was not serious, and had only spoken in the cups of which he was very fond. At this time Brentford was old and the King would have liked to promote Prince Rupert to Commander in Chief of the Royalist armies, but Rupert could not be spared in the north. However, Rupert did send Lord Goring south, and he reached Charles on 7 August. The King promptly dismissed Lord Wilmot and installed Goring in his stead, as Lieutenant General of the Horse, at the same time making Lord Hopton General of the Ordnance in place of Wilmot's friend Lord Percy. This was a very unpopular move all round and alienated some of Charles's senior supporters, apart from the fact that Wilmot was probably his best cavalry commander. Wilmot and Percy were exiled and went to France.

MAP 30

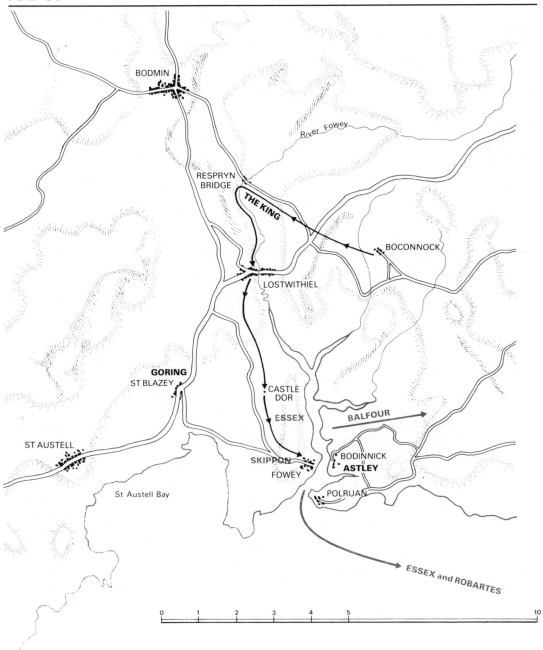

BODMIN

River Fowey

RESPRYN
BRIDGE

THE KING

BOCONNOCK

LOSTWITHIEL

GORING
ST BLAZEY

CASTLE
DOR

ESSEX

BALFOUR

ST AUSTELL

SKIPPON

BODINNICK

ASTLEY

FOWEY

POLRUAN

St Austell Bay

ESSEX and ROBARTES

0   1   2   3   4   5   10

MAP 30

The Battle of Lostwithiel

10 August–5 September 1644

ESSEX'S army numbered about 10,000 and the King's about 16,000 men even without Grenville. The Royalists moved nearer to Lostwithiel: Boconnock, three miles to the east, was occupied, Respryn bridge over the River Fowey two miles to the north of it was seized on 12 August, and thus Essex was cut off on the landward side. On 14 August Sir Jacob Astley took Bodinnick on the eastern side of the Fowey estuary and Polruan castle, making it impossible for Parliamentary ships to enter the harbour. On 21 August Grenville, having now joined the King, captured the ruined castle at Restormel and on the 26th Goring occupied St Blazey. Surrounded, Essex had insuperable problems and blamed everyone but himself for them.

Charles's army was still wide spread and much of it was busy foraging because he was in almost as bad a situation as Essex for provisions, and on 31 August, during a wet and stormy night, Sir William Balfour, with about 2,000 cavalry, broke through the ring. Although pursued by the Earl of Cleveland, he made his way to Plymouth without much loss. Also on that day the Royalists began their attack on Lostwithiel and soon occupied the town. Essex's foot slowly withdrew to an old earthwork known as Castle Dor where he had positioned his baggage train and his few guns in anticipation. Later in the day the Royalists attacked this position, and after hard fighting some of Essex's regiments broke. The King's troops poured through the gap so created, swung round and cut the road to Fowey.

Realising that no help was at hand and that defeat was inevitable, Essex put Skippon in command. With Lord Robartes he slipped into Fowey, boarded a small boat and escaped to Plymouth. This was seen by many as the action of a poltroon, not to have faced the music with his men, and he was much criticised for it. In fact he was no coward; and as Commander-in-Chief of the Roundhead armies, and one of their few component generals, it was perhaps a sensible decision.

On 2 September Skippon surrendered and his remaining 6,000 troops, hungry and weary, were disarmed and granted very generous terms, being allowed to march out under guard, promising not to fight again before they reached Southampton. Some tried to take their arms with them but the local population quickly put a stop to this with no great gentleness. Why Charles allowed them to leave and did not insist on taking the Parliamentary army prisoner en masse is hard to understand, although he had few men that could be spared to guard them and nothing with which to feed them. As a result, however, Parliament was able to minimise the disaster to its cause, although only about 1,000 men reached Southampton; the rest died of exposure, starvation and disease, many of them having virtually no clothing and all having been forced to march without food and shelter.

On 3 September Grenville recaptured Saltash, whilst the King advanced to Tavistock and then turned southwards to Plymouth and reinvested the port. (See Map 29.) By then Balfour and his horse were well on their way eastwards along the coast and Essex had also left for London, where he was censured by Parliament for his defeat.

MAP 31

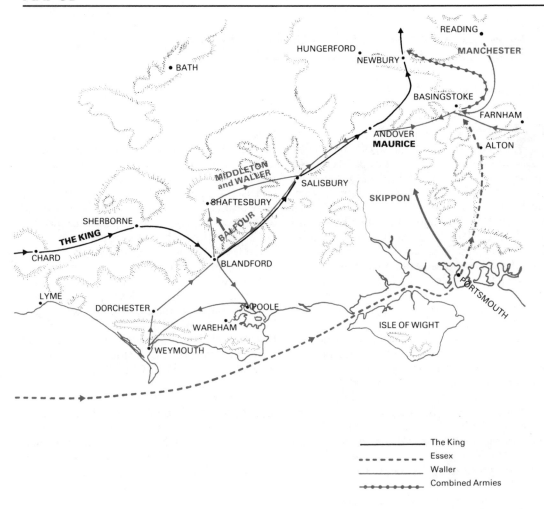

The King
CHARD
SHERBORNE
BATH
HUNGERFORD
NEWBURY
READING
MANCHESTER
BASINGSTOKE
FARNHAM
ANDOVER
MAURICE
ALTON
MIDDLETON and WALLER
SALISBURY
SHAFTESBURY
SKIPPON
BALFOUR
BLANDFORD
LYME
DORCHESTER
POOLE
WAREHAM
WEYMOUTH
ISLE OF WIGHT
PORTSMOUTH

——————— The King
– – – – – – Essex
——————— Waller
●–●–●–●–● Combined Armies

| 0 | 5 | 10 | 20 | 30 |

Charles Gerard, Earl of Macclesfield (c1620-1694)

A Lancashire man, he served in the Dutch army and then joined the Royalists. A bold and competent cavalry commander, he was wounded many times, and escaped abroad after the war. He returned at the Restoration, but his stormy career and friendship with Monmouth caused him to be outlawed, although he returned again with William of Orange. He lived to be the last surviving commander of the war.

Prince Maurice (1621-1652)

Son of the 'Winter Queen', Elizabeth of Bohemia, he accompanied his brother, Prince Rupert, to England in 1642. An intrepid horseman and a brave and skillful commander, he too often joined his troops in pillaging to be popular and was overshadowed by his brother. He died at sea in the West Indies.

MAP 31

Lostwithiel to Newbury

6 August–16 October 1644

ON 6 August Parliament exhorted Manchester to attack Rupert at Chester where he was recruiting a new army. But Manchester's army was not in very good shape, particularly on account of the antipathy between its commanders: Cromwell and Crawford, commander of the foot, were at enmity and Cromwell was contemptuous of Manchester himself and furious at his unwillingness to fight. So Manchester refused, on the somewhat specious grounds that it was too late in the year to mount a siege and that he would be very vulnerable on his journey from East Anglia, and on the very valid grounds that his troops would not fight so far from home.

However, when it was known that Rupert had set off southwards, the still unwilling Manchester started out and reached Huntingdon on 8 September. While spending a few days there, he learned of the disaster at Lostwithiel and now offered to do all he could to help. Cromwell meanwhile was trying to get Crawford dismissed, although in this he had no success.

Charles, after leaving Plymouth, marched towards Oxford because his army needed a rest, tired after its long marches and six months of campaigning; the King soon heard that detachments of his army had recaptured Barnstaple and Ilfracombe. His army was by now much reduced in size as he had suffered quite heavy casualties at Lostwithiel, and his arrangements for a new siege of Lyme and for a siege of Taunton left it weaker still, too weak in fact to meet the combined armies of Waller and Manchester. Rupert met him at Chard and was ordered to gather from Gloucestershire his 2,000 horse and the 2,000 foot under Charles Gerard. Charles hoped that this would induce the Roundheads to split and send a force to defend Gloucester, but if it did not Rupert was instructed to march to the King with all speed. He learned that Wareham had been captured by a Roundhead detachment and that Hurry, who had deserted from the Roundheads before Chalgrove Field, had now changed sides again!

Essex, back in the field, ordered Sir William Balfour to delay the Royalists at Blandford, but his patrols were badly worsted by Royalist cavalry. He withdrew to Shaftesbury where he joined up with Middleton's horse and with Waller, who was hoping that he could draw the King into battle there and cut him off from Oxford. Charles was not to be drawn and marched on to Sherborne, sending a detachment to relieve Portland. He also saw that he would have to relieve Banbury, Donnington castle and Basing House as soon as possible, all of which had been under siege for some time, and hurried on, reaching Salisbury on 15 October. There he learned that Waller had retired to Andover, and with Manchester at Reading called Rupert to his aid. However, Rupert had marched into Wales — again disobeying orders — and thus not being able to reach the King quickly another chance of a decisive Royalist victory was lost.

Manchester was still loath to move and both Waller and Cromwell despaired of any success while he was in command. On 22 September he was at Watford, and in the next three days he advanced just four miles, eventually reaching Reading on the 29th, and it was not until 16 October that he started for the west as ordered to help Waller. Philip Skippon was heading for Newbury from Portsmouth with the foot which had been released from Lostwithiel.

MAP 32

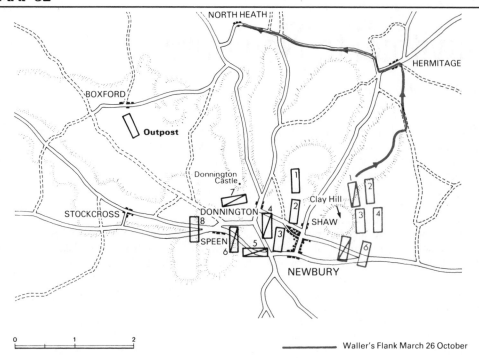

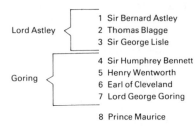

Waller's Flank March 26 October

0   1   2

Lord Astley	1 Sir Bernard Astley		1 Sir William Balfour
	2 Thomas Blagge		2 Earl of Manchester
	3 Sir George Lisle		3 Sir William Waller's Foot
Goring	4 Sir Humphrey Bennett		4 Philip Skippon
	5 Henry Wentworth		5 Oliver Cromwell
	6 Earl of Cleveland		6 Barclay
	7 Lord George Goring		
	8 Prince Maurice		

MAP 32

The Second Battle of Newbury (1)

17–27 October 1644

KING Charles met up with Waller again at Andover. Although his plans to attack him were foiled by Maurice's mismanagement, a strong body of horse charged Waller's outposts and scattered them to such effect that he withdrew to Basingstoke where he joined up with Manchester on 17 October. Charles was near Newbury on 22 October. The besiegers of Donnington castle withdrew and he prepared to deploy to the north of the town, basing his defensive line on Shaw, Donnington and Speen. He sent a detachment of horse and foot under the Earl of Northampton to relieve Banbury, which it did on 25 October. The King intended to hold a defensive position at Newbury if he could, to prevent the Roundheads from using the town as billets and to leave them exposed to the winter weather which was just beginning.

The Roundheads marched towards Newbury and deployed on the key ridge of Clay Hill to the northeast of the town, on which the Royalists, as at the first battle when they had omitted to hold Round Hill, had neglected to place any outposts. Manchester was now in command because Essex had left the field through illness and retired to Reading, which was a mixed blessing — although it solved the problem besetting Parliament as to who should be in command, since neither of them was willing to serve under the other.

The Royalist army, of about 12,000 men, consisted of the artillery under Lord Hopton and the horse under Lord George Goring, with brigades commanded by Goring himself, Wentworth, Cleveland and Sir Humphrey Bennett. The infantry was under Lord Astley (Sir Jacob having been raised to the peerage), the brigades being commanded by his son Sir Bernard Astley, Thomas Blagge and Sir George Lisle. Prince Maurice was at the rear at Speen, and early in the battle was told to face west and to throw up earthworks on Speen Hill in case of an attack from that direction, which was remarkably prescient since such an event must have seemed most unlikely. The army deployed on 25 October.

After probing manoeuvres by the Roundhead patrols on 25 October which failed to locate the main army positions, and a desultory artillery duel, it was agreed by the Roundhead commanders that the Royalist defences were too strong to attack successfully by frontal assault. They therefore decided on a very daring plan in which Waller was to take his army of about 12,000 men on a wide outflanking march, during the night, around the north of the Royalist position and attack from the west against the weaker rear defences, while Manchester with his remaining 7,000 men occupied the Royalist army with limited attacks from Clay Hill.

The danger was that the Roundhead army would be divided and if anything went wrong during the long and difficult night march and the manoeuvre was discovered, the Cavaliers would be able to attack and defeat Manchester and then turn to confront Waller with the whole army. Nevertheless, during the evening of 26 October Waller set off and halted for the night at North Heath.

MAP 33

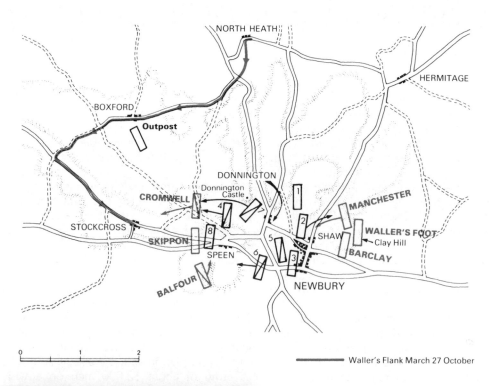

Scale: 0 — 1 — 2

Waller's Flank March 27 October

1 Sir Bernard Astley
2 Thomas Blagge
3 Sir George Lisle
4 Sir Humphrey Bennett
5 Henry Wentworth
6 Earl of Cleveland
7 Lord George Goring
8 Prince Maurice

Edward Montagu, Earl of Manchester (1602-1671)

A leading Parliamentary commander, he was a gentle and lethargic man, and not fitted to be a soldier: he believed in reconciliation rather than fighting. Although old friends, he was disparaged by Cromwell and deprived of command. He opposed the regicides and retired from public life, later greatly helping to bring about the Restoration.

MAP 33

The Second Battle of Newbury (2)

27 October 1644

EARLY on 27 October Waller's advance guard surprised a Royalist outpost at the ford at Boxford and defeated it after a hard fight, and his army marched on towards Speen. By now, apart from intelligence from Boxford, the columns of troops had been seen by the lookouts at Donnington castle and the Royalists knew that their rear was threatened, but it appears that the threat was not regarded as serious. Perhaps the strength of Waller's army was not appreciated since nothing was done about its approach; no reinforcements were sent against it and even Maurice was not told of the situation.

Manchester had attacked at dawn on 27 October towards Shaw House, but Astley delivered an immediate counter-attack and drove the Roundheads off in confusion; in spite of knowing by then that Manchester was much weakened, the counter-attack was not exploited. It was early afternoon when Waller eventually deployed, on high ground near Stockcross, with Skippon and the infantry in the centre, Balfour on the right and the main body of horse under Cromwell on the left.

Waller's attack took Maurice completely by surprise. However, his position was strong, the hedges and lanes made the approach difficult for the attackers, and the first assault was beaten off. But the second one was more successful, capturing some of the guns lost at Lostwithiel and sweeping into Speen. Balfour charged Maurice's cavalry which broke in disorder, then Cleveland countercharged with little success and was taken prisoner. Cromwell's cavalry on the left had somehow become delayed and were in some disarray, and when they appeared Goring and Bennett charged and drove them back in disorder. In the east Manchester, who it was intended should act in concert with Waller, at last attacked again. He was really too late because it was almost dark, and after some initial success and some heavy fighting was driven back by a furious counter-attack.

Night had now fallen, and neither side was happy about the situation, both believing that they had lost. The Royalists had probably had a slight edge on the battle and in any case remained in command of the battlefield. Nevertheless Charles, fearing another attack by Waller at Speen the following day, decided to retreat, and Astley made a masterly withdrawal of the army through Wallingford towards Oxford, leaving Donnington still besieged. The Roundheads had been hit very hard in the battle and had lost heavily, and were no doubt relieved to find in the morning that the Royalists had gone. In fact the battle, like so many others in the war, was indecisive, but the Royalists had lost a chance.

Waller pursued the Cavaliers for some distance but was recalled, in spite of Cromwell trying to urge Manchester to follow with the foot. Eventually Manchester agreed to move and set out, but again too late as the Royalists were nearing Oxford now, and the Roundhead army returned to Newbury.

On 7 November Charles and Rupert, who had been promoted to Commander-in-Chief in place of the aged Brentford, set out again from Oxford with 11,000 men to relieve Donnington castle; Manchester ordered Cromwell to stop him. This was an impossible task with the force available, and Charles pressed on and Donnington was relieved. Charles again drew up his army before Newbury, and the Roundheads were determined that he should not occupy Newbury itself, although by now their army was in a parlous state and very short of provisions. The Roundheads moved out of Newbury to Kingsclere to meet the King, but the troops had had enough and many vanished. Reluctantly the whole Roundhead army was forced to return to Reading, while Charles did nothing to stop them and entered Newbury.

MAP 34

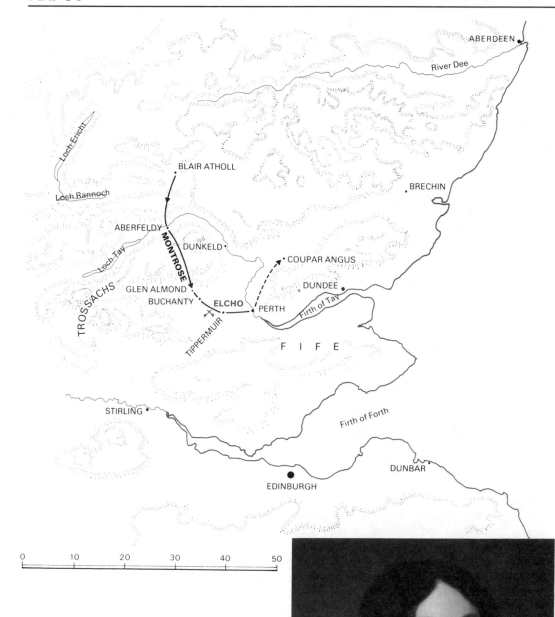

James Graham, Marquess of Montrose (1612-1650)

Son of a Scottish peer, he joined the Covenanters in 1639 and opposed Charles I. In 1644 he joined the Royalists and became commander of their army in Scotland. A brilliant soldier, particularly as a commander of irregular forces, he had a meteoric career until his defeat at Philiphaugh. Nevertheless, he continued fighting until finally overcome and betrayed. Still proclaiming his loyalty to the King, he was found guilty of treason by the Covenanters and hanged in Edinburgh.

MAP 34

Montrose's First March: Tippermuir

30 August–1 September 1644

THE Covenanters had three armies in Scotland: Lord Elcho was based in Perth to defend Fife and Edinburgh, Lord Balfour of Burleigh was in the north in Aberdeen, and the Marquess of Argyll was in the southwest, based on his home at Inverary. They had few worries about the Marquess of Montrose who they did not believe could assemble enough recruits from the Highlands to pose any sort of threat to them.

Having formed some sort of an army composed mostly of Irish regiments, and having raised his Standard, Montrose left Blair Atholl on 30 August. His intention was to defeat Elcho before Argyll could come to his aid, but he did not know where Argyll was or how long he had for his task. He marched south, past the western end of Loch Tummel, and approaching Aberfeldy had a fierce encounter at Castle Menzies with some of Argyll's supporters of that clan. Having subdued them he pushed on south to Glen Almond and then turned east towards Perth. At Buchanty he came into contact with Lord Kilpont, sent by Elcho to delay him, who promptly changed sides; the march continued southwards to Fowlis Moor where he spent the night.

On the following morning, 1 September, Elcho marched out from Perth. He took up a position at Tippermuir, about five miles west of the town, with about 8,000 men, much superior in numbers to Montrose's army but inferior in experience and quality. Elcho commanded the right wing himself, with Murray of Gask in the centre and Sir James Scott on the left, with horse on each flank. To give an impression of greater strength than he had and to prevent against being flanked, Montrose deployed his regiments thinly, that is each regiment in three lines instead of six, with the three Irish regiments in the centre, Kilpont on the left and the Atholl Highlanders on the right. The Highlanders were under his own command, and they were armed with stones because they did not have muskets. Montrose sent a messenger to Lord Elcho inviting him to support the King, but the messenger was taken prisoner.

Elcho attacked first with cavalry from his left wing, which were hit by heavy enfilade fire from the Irish, and by a shower of stones from the Atholls which panicked the horses. The cavalry broke and fled, devastating the infantry as they went. Taking advantage of the disorder Montrose attacked all along the line and the Covenanter foot fled in panic, only Scott standing for a short time until he too was driven off. Montrose's army, killing many in the rout, pursued to Perth which immediately surrendered. There he rested such of his army as remained; the Highlanders, having collected their share of the booty (which was basically why they had joined the battle), set off home. Montrose was to discover that, rather like the Trained Bands in England, this melting away after battle was an irritating habit of the Scots.

Montrose's victory caused minor consternation in Edinburgh and the Covenanters put a price on his head. Nevertheless, although some of Leven's army investing Newcastle was sent back to Scotland, the Scots were still confident of their superiority, and by now Argyll was approaching, albeit in leisurely fashion.

MAP 35

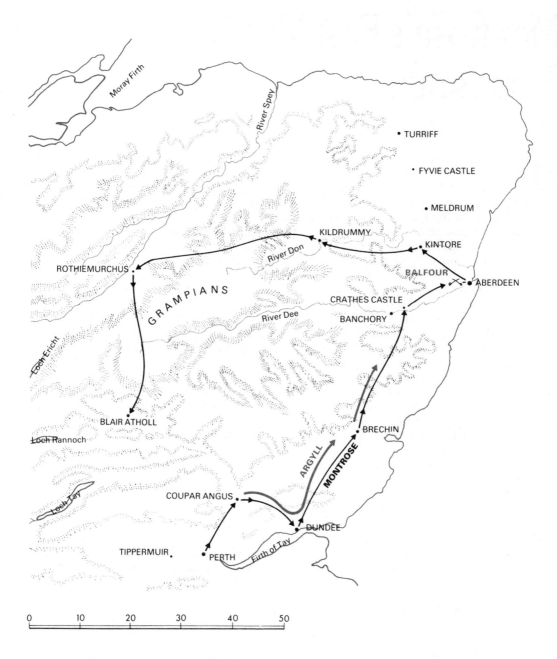

MAP 35

Montrose's First March: Aberdeen

4–13 September 1644

MONTROSE could not afford to let the two remaining Covenanter armies join up and on 4 September set off after Lord Balfour in Aberdeen before Argyll could catch him up. His route took him through Coupar Angus and Dundee (where he hoped to cause alarm merely by his presence although he did not attack the city) to Brechin, which he reached on 9 September. Argyll reached Perth on 11 September. Montrose was hoping to collect recruits on the way, but they were disappointingly few, although he was joined by Lord Airlie with 44 horse, which was a great bonus to his meagre force.

On 11 September Montrose seized Crathes castle neat Banchory on the River Dee, and the following day marched rapidly towards Aberdeen. Considering the conditions he was making remarkable progress at a speed of around 20 miles a day. Hearing of Montrose's coming, Burleigh marched his army of about 2,500 men out of the city on 13 September and deployed on a hill about a mile to the southwest. Montrose sent a drummer boy as an envoy to order the city to surrender, but this was refused and the poor little boy was shot by a Covenanter soldier; Montrose was so furious at this that he gave the Irish regiments leave to sack the city, which they subsequently did with much blood being spilt.

Again Montrose, his army only about 1,500 men strong apart from his 44 horse, deployed his Irish regiments in the centre. He put some horse on either flank, with Kilpont's men among them, although Kilpont himself had meanwhile been killed in a duel. Burleigh's dispositions were similar. The Irish moved forward, some of Burleigh's horse attacking ineffectually against Montrose's right. Burleigh attempted to outflank the Royalist left, and for a moment the situation looked dangerous, but again the attack was weak and was counter-attacked by Royalist horse which was moved across from the right flank.

Sir William Forbes of Craigeivar, seeing that the Royalist right was now devoid of horse, attacked the Irish and MacDonald's musketeers with cavalry. The Irish employed a neat ruse and opened their ranks to allow the horse to pass through them without doing much damage; they then turned about and unleashed a devastating fire on their rear which drove Forbes's horse from the field. Both of Burleigh's wings being now out of action, the Irish regiments attacked and the whole of the Covenanter army fled in panic.

Montrose had now defeated and badly mauled two of the Covenanter armies but was still not confident of taking on Argyll in the open. He left Aberdeen and marched northeast to Kintore, whilst Argyll, too late again, entered Aberdeen on 19 September. Montrose carried on to Alford and Kildrummy castle, hoping, but failing, to raise the Gordons to join him. In fact two of the Marquess of Huntly's sons were with the Covenanters — one had actually been with Burleigh at Aberdeen — because their mother was sister to Argyll, and Huntly himself regarded Montrose as of no importance since his estates were very small. Montrose now took to the mountains, marched on to Cock Bridge and, after crossing the Cairngorms, reached Rothiemurchus castle south of Aviemore on 3 October. From there he returned to Blair Atholl whence he had set out five weeks before.

MAP 36

MAP 36

Montrose's Second March: Fyvie Castle and Inverlochy

14 September 1644–3 February 1645

MONTROSE did not stay long at Blair, where he was a target for Argyll, but set off again, east and then north, across the rivers Dee and Don until he reached Fyvie castle, well north of Aberdeen and midway between Meldrum and Turriff. Argyll was still pursuing him, and having eventually caught up decided to attack the castle from the east, which was the only side which was not protected by bogs. Montrose chose his position well and formed up his small force on a bank which dominated Argyll's approach to the castle. Argyll attacked and after a desperate struggle Montrose's meagre force drove off the enemy with many casualties. Montrose slipped away again and made his way once more to Blair by the end of November. Winter campaigning was very difficult in the Highlands, and Argyll assuming that there would be no further action until the spring, made his way back to Edinburgh and then home.

Montrose and his Highlanders and Irish were made of sterner stuff. By now Mac-Donald, who commanded Antrim's Irish brigade, had returned with a number of recruits from the west, where he had been checking his bases. These reinforcements were mainly Camerons and MacDonalds who all hated Argyll and his Campbells. Montrose was persuaded by them to attack Argyll in his home country at Inverary at the northern end of Loch Fyne, and then set off across the snow covered mountains to destroy the Campbells. It was an avenging army as it marched southward, killing cattle, burning houses and putting any Campbell that it found to the sword, in the manner in which the Campbells had assaulted the other clans through the centuries. Montrose reached the county of Argyll on 13 December and, having created havoc but not actually having attacked Inverary, left again at the end of January 1645, marching northwards until he reached Loch Ness.

There Seaforth with 5,000 men barred his way. With Argyll behind him, including in his army two of Leven's regiments which had fought at Marston Moor, it seemed that Montrose might have fallen into a trap as he had only about 1,500 men himself. He retired down the Great Glen, and having made his way through the very rough country of the Corryarrick Pass, came up with Argyll at Inverlochy, where the Glen meets Loch Linnhe near the present-day Fort William. Argyll had given command of his army to Sir Duncan Campbell and himself slipped away, and Campbell placed his Highlanders in the centre with a newly recruited Lowland regiment on each flank.

On 2 February Montrose attacked with his whole force and the Lowland regiments broke immediately. Although the Campbells in the centre fought bravely they were no match for the ferocious enemy and at last they too broke. Nearly 1,700 of Argyll's army of 3,000, including Sir Duncan Campbell, were killed in the disaster, and the Campbells ceased for a while to be a power in the west.

Montrose was elated with his victory, which had now virtually destroyed the Covenanter armies in Scotland. Possibly overrating his own prowess in the process, he wrote to the King on 3 February of his high hopes for the future in Scotland, with him as its viceroy.

The Situation in Late 1644 and Early 1645

IN September 1644 Sir Thomas Middleton took Montgomery castle after a weak defence by Lord Herbert of Cherbury, and an attempt to retake it by Lord Byron on 18 September was defeated by a Roundhead force under Sir John Meldrum, thus leaving the Severn valley in Parliamentary hands. Meldrum moved north and besieged Liverpool which fell on 1 November, most of the English defenders defecting to the Roundheads and the Irish being made prisoner.

On 27 October Leven's Scots at last captured Newcastle, and occupied Tynemouth castle on 6 November. On 12 November Lord Fairfax took Helmsley castle and in December took Knaresborough castle. Meanwhile on 31 October the Cavaliers attempted to relieve Crowland, north of Peterborough, which they had captured earlier that month and then been besieged in the town. A Roundhead force appeared on the scene and the Royalists broke and fled in disorder — morale in that area must have been low.

In the southwest, Taunton had been besieged during the return of the Royalist army from Lostweithiel (see Map 31) and was now completely isolated. Although Waller was ordered to relieve the town in November he was too busy with other things and too weak to do so, and eventually in December the Roundhead General Holborn took a force through Dorset. He was supported by Sir Anthony Ashley Cooper who had raised a Royalist regiment after the battle of Roundway Down and been appointed governor of Portland and Weymouth, but in January 1644 had gone over to the Roundheads: in August he had taken part in the capture of Wareham, and had proved to be one of the most fanatical Roundhead supporters, giving little quarter in

any of his forays. On 14 December Taunton was relieved.

Early in 1644 Archbishop Laud, who it will be remembered was arrested with Strafford in 1641, had been brought to trial for treason. The trial dragged on for months. He was found guilty and executed on 10 January 1645, a few days after Sir John Hotham and his son (who had been prepared to surrender Hull to the Royalists, see Map 12).

Also on 10 January, having attempted and failed to take Abingdon by trying to persuade Browne to change sides, Charles attacked the town and the Royalists were driven back with heavy casualties. Lord George Goring carried out a series of raids in Hampshire and Surrey in January, actually occupying Waller's old base at Farnham, but he had not sufficient strength to remain there and defend the town and so withdrew again.

In February a detachment of Royalists had seized one of the forts at Weymouth after hard fighting and had put the town in danger. Waller was ordered to relieve it and, learning of this, the Royalists abandoned the siege — in fact Waller's cavalry had mutinied and refused to serve any longer under him. The major problem now with the Roundhead army was that there was no money with which to pay it, and so, living off the land as it had to do, it was alienating many Parliamentary supporters.

In spite of the situation in the London area and the south, the Parliamentary cause was flourishing in other parts of the country. On 22 February the Royalist garrison of Shrewsbury was surprised and defeated, and at the same time Sir John Meldrum managed to reduce and capture Scarborough; the castle there still held out, and subsequently in early May Sir John was mortally wounded trying to take it. In the southwest the Royalist incursion at Weymouth was heavily defeated on 28 February, but in March, Goring, without authority, set off on another of his forays, this time into the southwest. On 11 March he besieged Taunton again, but a party of horse coming to his support was devastated by Cromwell and Waller near Devizes. However, Goring caught up with Cromwell's horse near Dorchester and routed them with heavy losses.

In the northwest Rupert was attempting to join up with his brother, Maurice, who was at Chester with Byron, gaining further dislike by plundering the surrounding countryside. Although Rupert raised the Roundhead siege of Beeston castle he was unable to progress into Lancashire — where he might have collected more recruits, as he had before Marston Moor — because Roundhead troops under Sir David Leslie were soon dispatched to stop him. At Hereford the local inhabitants rose against the Royalist depredations and Rupert had to return to make peace with them. More and more the populace was showing its lack of support for either side in the struggle.

In the Parliamentary army the animosities which had arisen after the battle of Marston Moor had continued. Cromwell and Manchester were still at loggerheads. Cromwell, who was a rabid Puritan and hated the established church, believed that the war must be won by defeating the King absolutely, which to him meant not only changing the Constitution and creating a republic, but also purging the church of what he considered was idolatry. Manchester on the other hand believed that the war must be won but with reconciliation, stating that if the King was beaten 99 times he was still King and they were still his subjects, but if the Roundheads were beaten once they would be hanged.

Parliament now believed that the failures in 1644 before Marston Moor had been largely due to the ineptness of Essex and Manchester, and Cromwell proposed that all Members of Parliament should resign from their military posts — the Self Denying Ordinance — which would of course include both Essex and Manchester who were hereditary members of the House of Lords.

The Parliamentary New Model Army, authorised to comprise 22,000 men, was now being formed, and on 21 January Sir Thomas Fairfax was named as its Commander-in-Chief with Skippon as his Major General, although Parliament retained the right (against Cromwell's wish) to appoint officers to the army. The command of the horse was left vacant for the time being, as Parliament wanted to appoint Cromwell, but he was a Member of Parliament and subject also to the Self Denying Ordinance. The nominal strength of regiments of foot was approximately 1,000 men and that of regiments of horse approximately 500 men. Nevertheless, few regiments were often up to strength.

Early in April Essex and Manchester resigned their commissions, followed by Warwick as Lord High Admiral and by Waller: the Parliamentary army was falling more and more into the hands of Fairfax and Cromwell.

Archibald Campbell, Marquess of Argyll (1607-1661)

A Scottish Covenanter, he commanded one of the three Scottish armies until he was defeated by Montrose. He crowned Charles II at Scone, but after the Restoration he was found guilty of treason and beheaded in Edinburgh.

Sir Marmaduke (Lord) Langdale (1598-1661)

As High Sheriff of Yorkshire he refused to levy Ship Money, but nevertheless joined the Royalists at the outbreak of war. A good and brave commander of horse he escaped to France after the capitulation, although he returned with Charles II and was captured at Preston. He again escaped overseas, returning at the Restoration, but as a Catholic was given no important positions.

MAP 37

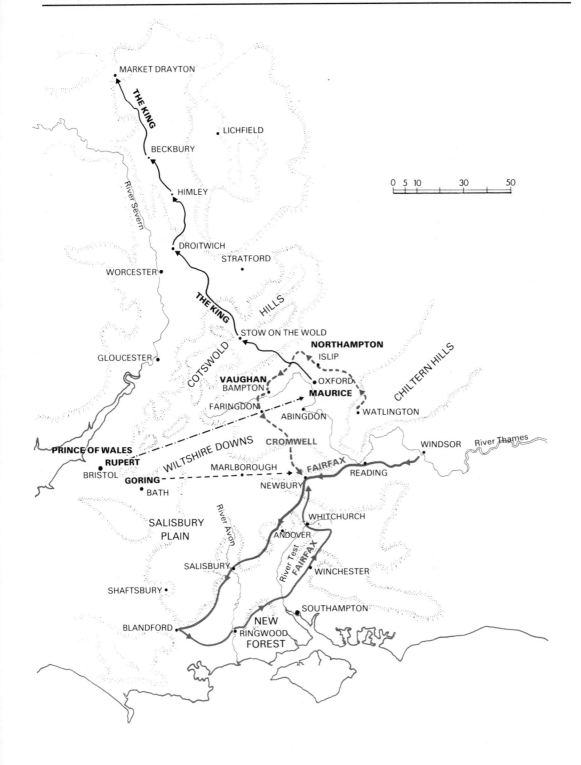

MAP 37

First Operations of the New Model Army

April–22 May 1645

I N EARLY April Rupert arrived at Bristol, where the Prince of Wales, not yet 15, had set up his Court and headquarters as Captain General in the West. Goring, who was earning an evil name in the southwest for his cruelty and extortion, was ordered to hand over his infantry and artillery to Sir Richard Grenville and to patrol the Wiltshire Downs with his cavalry to prevent the enemy incursions into the area, and particularly to prevent any interference with the siege of Taunton. Goring refused, left his command and retired to Bath.

Charles was now preparing to join Rupert to relieve Gloucester, and Cromwell was ordered to move west of Oxford to prevent this junction taking place, marching from Watlington on 23 April to attack the Earl of Northampton at Islip. Northampton had in fact left to collect reinforcements when Cromwell arrived, and returning on the following day was routed with heavy losses. Cromwell bypassed Oxford and attacked Sir William Vaughan at Bampton, and although he could not persuade Faringdon castle to surrender, he created havoc in the countryside and stopped any move westward by the King. Maurice had arrived at Oxford to lead the artillery to Gloucester but Cromwell soon stopped this by collecting up all the draught horses in the area.

The King appealed to Montrose to help him by marching south, but the latter's success at Inverlochy had caused Parliament to send an army to Scotland under Baillie and the renegade Hurry. Rupert wanted to destroy this force before it could reach Scotland and urged the King to join him, but Charles could not move out of Oxford. Goring had by now rejoined his horse and was ordered to set off with them, estimated at 2,000, for Oxford.

Fairfax, at Windsor, was ordered to relieve Taunton with such regiments of the New Model Army as were ready, and set out. He met Cromwell at Newbury, but that night some of Cromwell's horse were surprised by Goring and surrounded, and Rupert and Maurice reached Oxford with 2,000 foot and horse. Fairfax was in difficulties but obeyed orders and continued on his way. On 7 May he reached Blandford with his whole army, although why it was felt necessary to take 11,000 men to raise a siege is not obvious. At Blandford he was told to halt because of the situation at Oxford, but nevertheless sent a force to Taunton. The besiegers had recently attacked the town and set fire to part of it, but hearing of the approaching Roundheads they rapidly broke the siege.

Rupert again urged Charles to march northwards to join up with Montrose, and to send Goring (whom he disliked) back to the west; other counsel urged the King to attack Fairfax and eliminate him first while his regiments were still raw and untrained. Charles moved northward. On 11 May he reached Droitwich, and continued on to Market Drayton where on 22 May he heard that Brereton had abandoned the siege of Chester; it appeared that he was taking the right course of action.

MAP 38

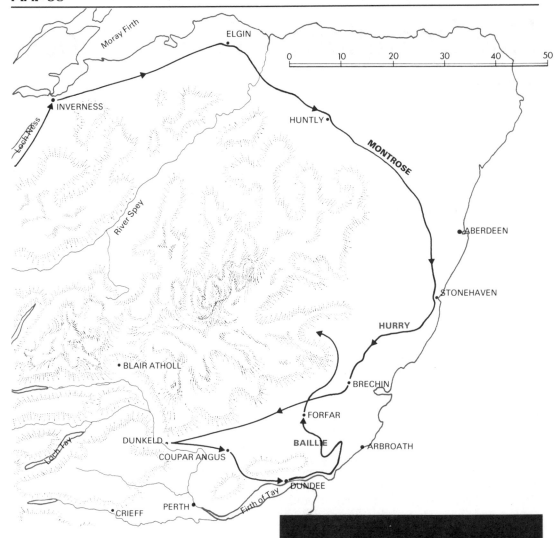

Moray Firth

ELGIN

INVERNESS

Loch Ness

HUNTLY

MONTROSE

ABERDEEN

River Spey

STONEHAVEN

HURRY

BLAIR ATHOLL

BRECHIN

FORFAR

DUNKELD

BAILLIE

ARBROATH

COUPAR ANGUS

Loch Tay

DUNDEE

Firth of Tay

CRIEFF

PERTH

0   10   20   30   40   50

King Charles II (1630-1685)

He was born in 1630 and, like his father, became heir
apparent on the death of his elder brother, and was
created Prince of Wales. During Cromwell's Protectorate
he lived in exile abroad and returned in 1660 to take up
his crown, until then only recognised by Scotland. At the
Restoration he did not intend to challenge Parliament or
the power of Puritanism, and was personally tolerant, but
he was not strong enough to control the Cavalier element
in the new Parliament. However, to be independent of
Parliament, which was his ideal, he founded the first
Standing Army in Britain. He was over fond of gaiety and
high living and was a dissolute man. Although he had no
children by his wife, Catherine of Braganza, daughter of
the King of Portugal, he had many by his numerous
mistresses, and his offspring founded a number of ducal
and other noble families still extant today. He died young,
in 1685.

MAP 38

Montrose's Third March: Dundee

February–5 April 1645

AFTER the battle of Inverlochy in February, Montrose rested his Irishmen who were tired after months of marching and fighting, his Highlanders having mostly gone home with their loot. He then turned back towards the Seaforths who had been blocking his way on Loch Ness, but they had melted away in the face of the man who had conquered the Campbells. Montrose marched on to Elgin and there, to his delight, he was joined by Lord Gordon, the eldest son and heir of the Marquess of Huntly. Lord Gordon had been rejected by the Covenanters and brought with him a small body of horse without which Montrose did not dare to venture into the Lowlands. Other waverers, the Seaforths and Grants, followed Gordon's example and also came to him for pardon, although, as proved to be right, Montrose did not entirely trust them.

Montrose had no funds with which to pay his troops and allowed them to live off the lands of the northern Covenanters: this was obviously unpopular and he was declared guilty of treason and exommunicated. Montrose continued southwards, still hoping (in vain) for help with horse from the King, and found that an army under Baillie and Hurry had entered Scotland to chase him. He burned the Covenanter stronghold of Stonehaven, and when Hurry, who had been following him at a distance, dared to attack his advance guard, a concealed Irish regiment repelled him with heavy casualties. Montrose next came up with Baillie (advancing from Perth) in Forfarshire and considerable manoeuvring resulted as neither side was keen to have a battle. Eventually, near Coupar Angus, Montrose challenged Baillie to fight, but Baillie refused, turned and retreated.

The manoeuvring had not been popular with the Highlanders, who preferred a good fight with plenty of plunder. As they already had spoils from Stonehaven, Brechin and Dunkeld which had been sacked, they began to melt away as usual. Even the Gordons were unhappy that he had not lived up to his reputation of Inverlochy with a battle. His hope for a march into the Lowlands, carrying all before him and getting recruits from those disenchanted with the Covenanters, faded away.

Montrose now turned on Dundee and occupied the city on 4 April, but found that Baillie, who had spread false reports on his whereabouts, had also turned and was again only a mile away. He marched out of the city as Baillie marched in, and took up a defensive position with his by now tiny force. Baillie charged him and was repulsed, and in the dark Montrose set off in retreat to the north towards Arbroath, with Baillie marching on a parallel course in the hope of cutting him off against the sea. Montrose was a brilliant tactician, and before he reached Arbroath he halted and retraced his steps for a short distance, then cut across Baillie's tail and headed for Brechin.

MAP 39

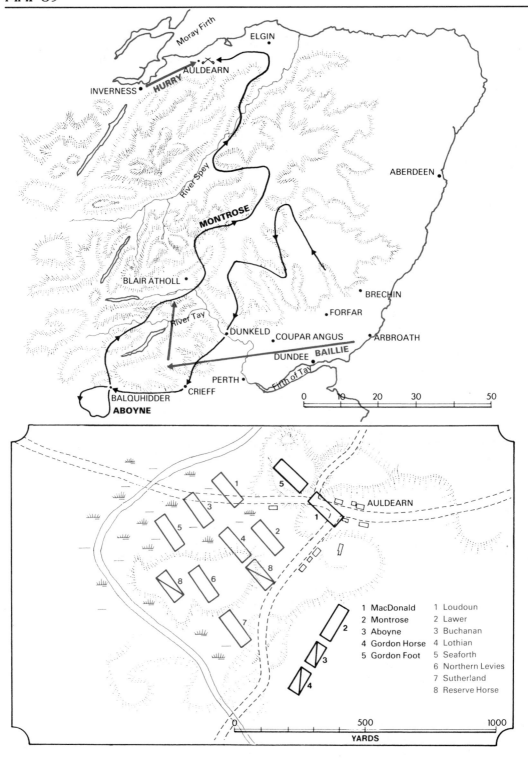

1 MacDonald
2 Montrose
3 Aboyne
4 Gordon Horse
5 Gordon Foot

1 Loudoun
2 Lawer
3 Buchanan
4 Lothian
5 Seaforth
6 Northern Levies
7 Sutherland
8 Reserve Horse

MAP 39

Montrose's Fourth March: Auldearn

5 April–9 May 1645

BAILLIE was unaware of Montrose's change of direction, and marched steadily onwards, by now well ahead. Then he realised his error and sent Hurry's cavalry after Montrose, who by that time had reached the safety of the mountains where Baillie and his horse dared not follow.

The march continued, Montrose turning south again through Dunkeld and Crieff to Balquhidder. There on 20 April he heard that Baillie had divided his army, Hurry driving north to cut him off from the Gordons. Montrose reached the Trossachs where he was joined by Lord James Aboyne, who had escaped from the siege of Carlisle, but, being threatened by Baillie once more, he decided to follow Hurry and turned north again. Hurry had reached Inverness, and there he was joined by various clans including Lovat, Sutherland and the Seaforths (who had changed sides again), and his army was now much larger than Montrose's. Montrose descended the Spey valley, at Elgin turned west towards Hurry, and on 8 May reached the village of Auldearn.

Hurry had come out from Inverness to find Montrose and to lead him into hostile country, which he had done, and he now turned back to face him. After a wet and windy night some of Hurry's soldiers fired their muskets to clear the damp powder from them, and Montrose, who up till then had no idea of Hurry's position, was now warned. He drew up his little force on a north-south line in front of the village, where the stone walls helped him as

barricades and the ground sloped away down to a marsh. MacDonald and his Irishmen were on a hill to the north and Montrose with his main force and horse was on the south of the village concealed on the reverse slope of a ridge. There was nothing in the centre but a few men who kept up a rapid fire to give the impression that the village was held strongly by Montrose. He hoped that Hurry would fall into his trap and attack MacDonald with his whole force, thus leaving his right flank unprotected.

On 9 May MacDonald was attacked by Hurry and, outnumbered, was forced back and on the point of being driven from the field or destroyed. Montrose, seeing what was going on but not being sure of Gordon's willingness to get too involved in the battle, employed a little deception and suggested that Gordon would not like all the honours of the battle to go to MacDonald, and that he should participate himself. Gordon accepted the challenge and charged Hurry's horse which broke and fled. Gordon now turned on Hurry's infantry and Montrose came from his hide with his foot to help. Hurry and his horse fled and his infantry were slaughtered where they stood.

It was a brilliant victory by so few over overwhelming odds, but the forces employed were so small that it was not a more widely decisive engagement. Baillie was still at large in Atholl which he had been ravaging while Montrose was otherwise engaged.

MAP 40

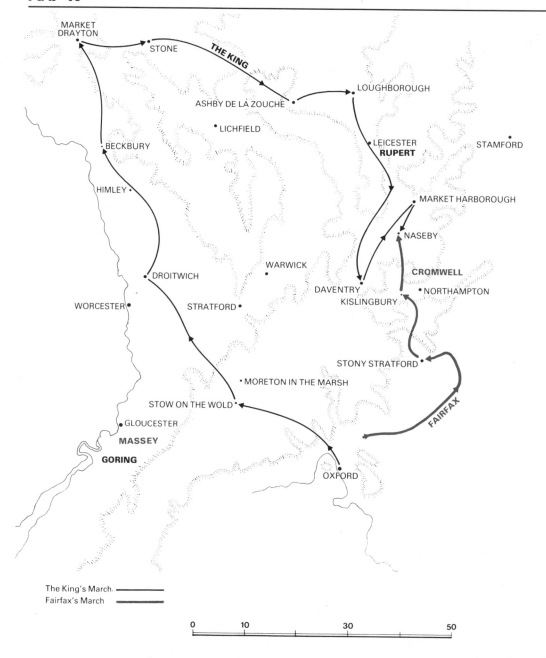

MARKET DRAYTON
STONE
THE KING
ASHBY DE LA ZOUCHE
LOUGHBOROUGH
LICHFIELD
BECKBURY
LEICESTER
RUPERT
STAMFORD
HIMLEY
MARKET HARBOROUGH
NASEBY
WARWICK
DROITWICH
CROMWELL
• NORTHAMPTON
WORCESTER
STRATFORD
DAVENTRY
KISLINGBURY
STONY STRATFORD
• MORETON IN THE MARSH
STOW ON THE WOLD
FAIRFAX
• GLOUCESTER
MASSEY
GORING
OXFORD

The King's March. ─────────
Fairfax's March   ━━━━━━━━━

0   10   30   50

Phillip Skippon (c1600-1660)

Born in Norfolk, he served abroad as a young man. Having joined the Parliamentarians he was largely responsible for the competence of the Trained Bands of London and served the Roundheads faithfully. He was a courageous, efficient soldier, who was always a friend to his troops.

Sir John Meldrum (1585-1645)

Born in Scotland he became a professional soldier. Returning to England he embraced a number of lucrative ventures, including the erection of lighthouses. He joined the Parliamentarians and was a successful and courageous leader, being killed at the siege of Scarborough.

MAP 40

The Prelude to Naseby

11 May–14 June 1645

WITH the King marching northwards the Roundheads also started to take positive action. Leven and his Scots were ordered to march south to meet the King, and Fairfax was ordered to besiege Oxford, where he arrived with Cromwell on 22 May. But Leven did not get far, as news had now reached him from Scotland of Montrose's victory at Auldearn and he returned into Westmoreland to prevent the junction between the King and Montrose.

Goring's expedition in the southwest and at Taunton had had no success, and he was ordered to return to Oxford, but Parliament realised that he must be kept busy in the west for as long as possible to prevent him from returning to join up with Charles. It therefore appointed Massey, who was in the Gloucester area, to lead a force towards Taunton, but before he left for his assignment he assaulted Evesham and captured it, putting a barrier between Charles and his base. The King was hoping that Oxford could hold out against siege while he was away.

Rather than run into Leven, Charles decided to take the eastern route to Scotland and turned into Staffordshire, from where he could go either north or south as occasion demanded. It had been agreed that he would combine forces with Goring and Rupert in Leicestershire; while waiting for this junction Rupert attacked Leicester and on 31 May captured the city by storm, sacking it brutally.

Again there was dissent in the Royalist councils as to which direction to head, some opting for a further march towards Yorkshire and others for a return to Oxford, which was in difficulties. The latter advice was accepted and on 7 June the Royalists entered Daventry whereupon the siege of Oxford was raised. Fairfax marched northeast and near Stony Stratford received reinforcements which increased his army to about 13,000 men. It was clear that a battle must soon take place in the vicinity.

Fairfax reached Kislingbury, about eight miles from Daventry on the Northampton road, on 12 June. That afternoon his cavalry clashed with Royalist outposts on Borough Hill, Charles having had no idea that the Roundheads were so close to him, and anyway having great contempt for the New Model Army. Both armies now marched northwards, Charles to the area of Market Harborough, while Fairfax was joined again by Cromwell and his horse. The King and Rupert would have preferred to put more distance between themselves and the Roundheads, but Fairfax was advancing fast and they concluded that the best action would be to fight him. Charles turned south to meet the Roundheads and both armies started to deploy.

The Royalists deployed initially on 14 June on a hill about two miles south of Market Harborough, which was Astley's chosen position as it would have entailed the Roundheads attacking uphill, particularly an advantage because the King was considerably outnumbered. There was no sign of the enemy and nothing happened.

MAP 41

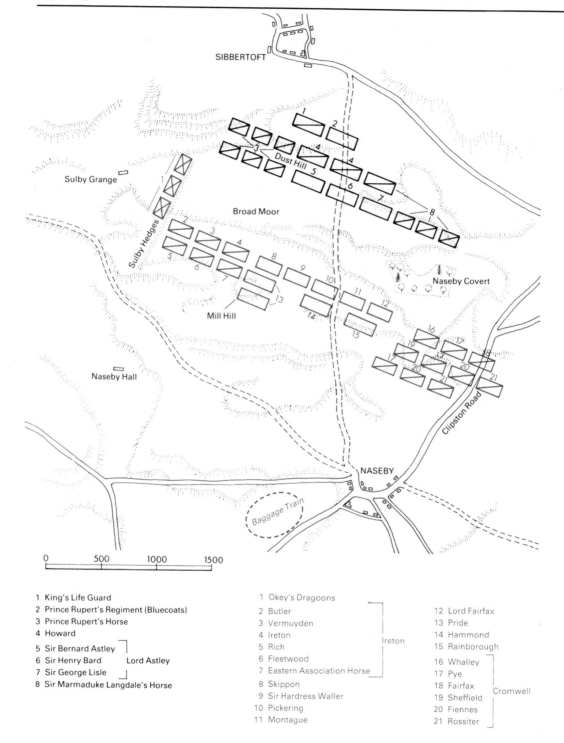

SIBBERTOFT

Dust Hill

Sulby Grange

Broad Moor

Sulby Hedges

Mill Hill

Naseby Covert

Naseby Hall

Clipston Road

NASEBY

Baggage Train

0   500   1000   1500

1 King's Life Guard
2 Prince Rupert's Regiment (Bluecoats)
3 Prince Rupert's Horse
4 Howard
5 Sir Bernard Astley ⎤
6 Sir Henry Bard   Lord Astley
7 Sir George Lisle ⎦
8 Sir Marmaduke Langdale's Horse

1 Okey's Dragoons
2 Butler
3 Vermuyden
4 Ireton
5 Rich
6 Fleetwood
7 Eastern Association Horse
8 Skippon
9 Sir Hardress Waller
10 Pickering
11 Montague

Ireton

12 Lord Fairfax
13 Pride
14 Hammond
15 Rainborough
16 Whalley
17 Pye
18 Fairfax
19 Sheffield
20 Fiennes
21 Rossiter

Cromwell

MAP 41

The Battle of Naseby (1)

14 June 1645

AFTER the Royalists had deployed, a scout sent out to look for Fairfax somewhat unaccountably reported that he could not be found, and Rupert set out himself to search for him — hardly the job for a Commander-in-Chief. He found the Roundhead army, and although he first thought it in retreat, in fact the Roundheads had first deployed between Chipston and Market Harborough and were now taking up new positions on better ground just north of the village of Naseby.

The new Parliamentary positions were on a ridge, with a marshy valley in front throught which it would have been difficult to charge with cavalry, even if had not been raining hard of late. Why the Royalists left their chosen position to conform to the Roundheads is not clear, but it may have been that Rupert, misunderstanding the redeployment, thought that he could attack with advantage while the enemy was disorganised. Whatever the reason, the Royalists moved forward and Rupert, seeing the marshy valley, deployed them on Dust Hill to the right of the Parliamentary front. The latter, in danger of being outflanked, changed their line to conform.

Unfortunately for Charles, Lord George Goring and his experienced horse had not arrived in time for the battle. The Cavaliers had between 7,500 and 10,000 men (no sure figure is available), and the Roundheads about 13,500 in a strong position in the hilly, undulating countryside. Philip Skippon, commanding the foot in the centre, had first deployed on top of the ridge but Fairfax had moved the line back to behind the brow, where his full strength could not be seen.

Ireton was with his horse on the left flank and Cromwell on the right, partly beyond the marshy area with open ground covered with furze in front of him. The dragoons were positioned on the left of the battlefield to be, behind the Sulby Hedges at right angles to the main line, so that they would have an uninterrupted field of fire on the flank of any cavalry charging towards the main position. Just before the battle began Cromwell gained an extra bonus when Rossiter joined him with 500 horse. As usual the Puritans in the Roundhead army vocally put their faith in God to provide them with the victory to which they thought they were entitled.

On the Royalist side Astley commanded the foot in the centre, the King was with the reserve to his rear, Rupert and Maurice were on the right wing and Sir Marmaduke Langdale, with his Yorkshiremen who were still discontented at being so far from home, was on the left. Both armies were tired after all the marching of recent weeks.

The Royalists advanced across the Broad Moor and up the hill, Rupert who had suffered from the fire of Okey's dragoons on the way, striking first against Ireton and being driven back. By then the infantry had clashed on the hill and the Roundheads were being driven back.

MAP 42

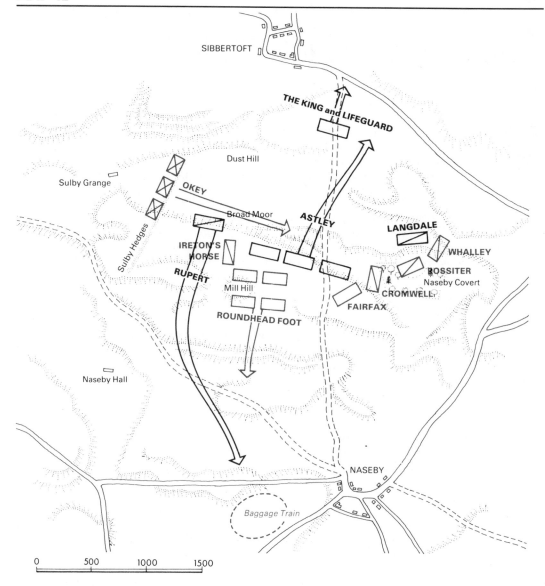

SIBBERTOFT

THE KING and LIFEGUARD

Dust Hill

Sulby Grange

OKEY

Broad Moor

ASTLEY

LANGDALE

WHALLEY

IRETON'S HORSE

ROSSITER

Naseby Covert

RUPERT

Mill Hill

CROMWELL

FAIRFAX

ROUNDHEAD FOOT

Naseby Hall

NASEBY

Baggage Train

0   500   1000   1500

MAP 42

The Battle of Naseby (2)

14 June 1645

HAVING driven back the first assault Ireton, ignoring the cavalry battle, turned to attack the Royalists now on his flank, but was wounded and made a prisoner. Rupert took advantage of the melee to charge the Roundhead horse on the left again, and this time drove them back in confusion. As usual Rupert did not stop to see what was happening elsewhere and pursued the fleeing horse round the rear of the Roundhead army until he reached the baggage train just outside Naseby. Having been brought up short by musket fire he reined in and turned back to the main battle, but he had again committed his sin of Edgehill — and far greater this time because he was Commander-in-Chief and should never have been leading the horse as he did. He had certainly contributed to a Royalist defeat, and had possibly thrown away a great possibility of victory.

In the infantry fight in the centre Skippon was also badly wounded, but would not leave the field although he could contribute nothing useful by remaining. The foremost regiments of the left and centre of the Parliamentary army, with the departure of Ireton's cavalry leaving them unprotected on the flank, fell back in disorder.

On the Parliamentary right Cromwell had waited, and seeing the Royalist foot and horse struggling on the slope of the hill and still gaining advantage, now charged their flank. Whalley and Rossiter hit Langdale's regiment, which had very difficult wet ground to cross as it advanced, and after a fierce battle routed it, leaving the Royalist left exposed.

Cromwell had an overwhelming advantage now and his horse again charged the Royalist regiments, supported by Fairfax's regiment of foot which had so far been little engaged. As the Roundheads advanced, the Royalists, including the reserve with the King, retreated. Okey's dragoons mounted and charged the Royalist right flank, adding to the confusion and panic. By the time that Rupert returned to battle all was lost; his small body of horse was powerless to attack the Roundhead might in the flush of victory. Fairfax drew up his line again, probably more or less where the Royalist position was at the start of the battle; the threat was too great and the Cavalier horse and foot fled.

It was a decisive victory because the Royalist infantry were almost annihilated; a comparatively small number had been killed, most being captured, but what made it worse was that of these 500 were officers — even if Charles could recruit new regiments he would not be able to find sufficient officers to command them. The artillery and almost the whole of the Royalist baggage train was also taken. Charles rode off through Leicester and halted at Ashby de la Zouche for the night, whilst Fairfax retook Leicester four days later. (As a sidelight on the battle, among those who suffered most were the Royalist 'camp followers', really a mobile brothel. The Puritans, being intolerant of any such vice, massacred many of them and branded the rest so that the harlots could never again follow their profession.)

The war was effectively over although it dragged on for another year.

MAP 43

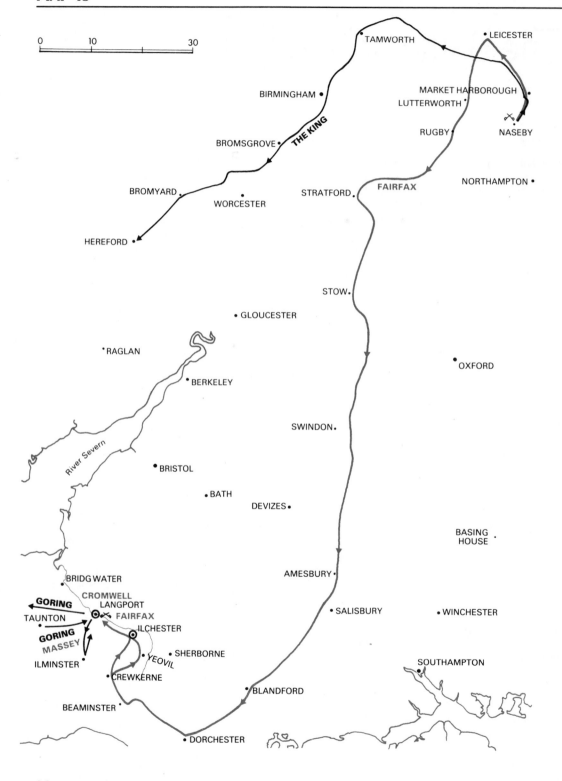

MAP 43

The Action at Langport

16 June–10 July 1645

ON 16 June 1645 Parliament confirmed Cromwell as Lieutenant General of Horse, and at the same time Sir William Beresford and Sir Thomas Middleton as commanders of the Parliamentary forces in Cheshire and North Wales respectively. On 18 June Leicester had surrendered to Fairfax who was then free to pursue the King. In spite of Montrose's victories in Scotland it was known that his force was small and it was believed that Baillie could contain him, and Leven's Scottish army was thus available to help in England.

Charles was by now at Hereford and hoped that Goring would soon be able to capture Taunton, which he was still besieging, and join him. Together they would have a strong army, and in addition the King was still hopeful of obtaining a large number of recruits from Ireland. In fact nothing was as rosy as he hoped. On 28 June Carlisle, after a very long siege surrendered to Sir David Leslie, and Leven began to march southwards to lay siege to Hereford.

Also in June Parliament had decided that Taunton must be freed and Fairfax set off for the southwest with his army: on 1 July he was near Salisbury, the next day at Blandford and at Dorchester on 3 July. In Devon Sir Richard Grenville had proved to be greedy and unscrupulous and was relieved of his command of the force besieging Plymouth. Replaced by Sir John Berkeley, he joined Goring, who was not much less greedy and was in addition dissolute. Meanwhile Goring, on the approach of the Roundhead army, had given up the siege of Taunton and retreated. Fairfax had followed a southerly route through Beaminster and on 5 July he first encountered the enemy at Crewkerne, drove off a cavalry outpost and learned that Goring held the bridges over the River Yeo at Ilchester and Langport, from where he could retreat to the stronghold of Bridgwater if necessary.

Fairfax decided to outmanoeuvre him and divided his force between Ilchester and Yeovil. Goring, being no strategist, did not take advantage of a divided enemy, having in fact already sent his baggage and most of his guns to Bridgwater, and then abandoned the bridge at Ilchester, leaving Fairfax with free passage. As a deception Goring had departed Langport with a body of horse ostensibly for Taunton again, and Fairfax sent Massey after him. Massey found Goring near Ilminster, scattered his force and Goring returned to the apparent safety of Langport. Fairfax crossed the River Yeo at Ilchester and on 10 July came into contact with Goring at Langport.

Goring had a strong position but only two guns, and Fairfax soon silenced them with a bombardment. To engage Goring, Fairfax would then have to advance across a deep and narrow ford and down a narrow, hedge-lined lane, with Goring's horse on the hill above him, which Goring thought would be sufficient deterrent. Nevertheless, two valiant bodies of Roundhead horse charged across the ford and, supported by musketeers, attacked the Royalist horse. At first they were checked, but with the arrival of another body of Roundhead horse Goring's army broke and fled. Cromwell now entered the battle and pursued the fleeing Royalists, overcoming them. Goring's army had to all intents ceased to exist, and he retired to Barnstaple with the few remaining men.

MAP 44

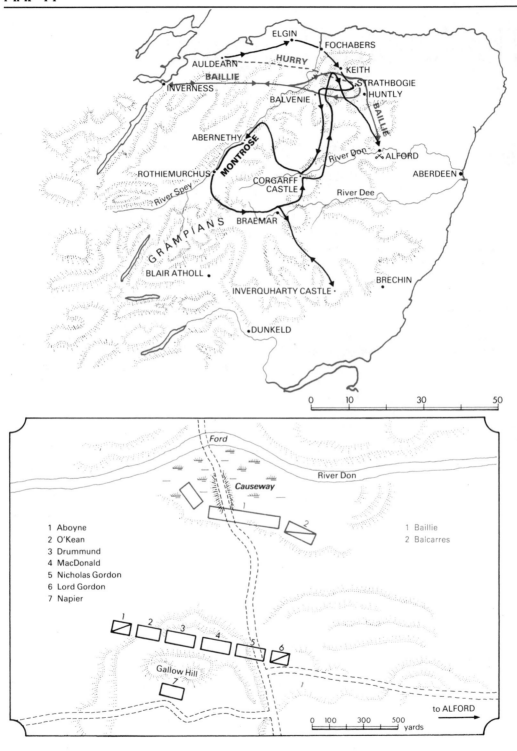

ELGIN

FOCHABERS

AULDEARN

HURRY

BAILLIE

KEITH

STRATHBOGIE

INVERNESS

HUNTLY

BALVENIE

BAILLIE

ABERNETHY

MONTROSE

River Don

ALFORD

ROTHIEMURCHUS

ABERDEEN

CORGARFF
CASTLE

River Dee

River Spey

G R A M P I A N S

BRAEMAR

BLAIR ATHOLL

INVERQUHARTY CASTLE

BRECHIN

DUNKELD

0   10   30   50

Ford

River Don

Causeway

1

2

1 Aboyne
2 O'Kean
3 Drummund
4 MacDonald
5 Nicholas Gordon
6 Lord Gordon
7 Napier

1 Baillie
2 Balcarres

1   2   3   4   5   6

Gallow Hill

7

to ALFORD →

0   100   300   500 yards

MAP 44

The Battle of Alford

10 May–2 June 1645

IN spite of his great victory at Auldearn, Montrose was still numerically very inferior to Baillie, particularly as his Highlanders had once more left him. After the battle the remnants of Hurry's horse had retreated to Strathbogie and joined up with Baillie. Montrose marched through Fochabers to Huntly, where Baillie tried to engage him, but, not wanting a battle in his weakened state, Montrose bypassed and outmanoeuvred him. He next returned west to Balvenie and ascended the valley of the Spey to Abernethy where Baillie dared not attack him. Baillie now returned to Inverness to obtain supplies. Montrose, free of him for the time being, therefore carried out an expedition against the new regiments which the Earl of Lindsay was recruiting. He marched via Rothiemurchus and Braemar and came up with Lindsay near Inverquharty castle, not far from Forfar, but Lindsay did not stay and fight, and retired southwards.

Montrose could do little in the area, and so returned across the hills to the ruins of Corgarff castle. There he was protected by the mountains, and awaited the return of Lord Gordon and MacDonald, who had left to collect the runaway Highlanders and anybody else that they could recruit. Baillie was ordered to hand over 1,000 of his men to Lindsay who could then approach Montrose from the south with experienced troops, but Lindsay, having obtained these reinforcements, set off to carry on the ravages of Atholl which Baillie had started.

Lord Gordon now returned with the deserters and Montrose set off north to find Baillie, which he did in a strong position near Keith. Baillie declined the challenge of a battle, so Montrose bypassed him and took up a strong position of his own on the Gallowhill ridge south of Alford, where Baillie was bound to follow or leave the road open to the Lowlands. On 2 July Montrose deployed his force, with his infantry in the centre, Aboyne's horse on the left and Gordon's on the right, again making use of the reverse slopes of the hill for concealment of part of the force. Baillie would have to cross the river by the ford, make his way over some marshy ground by a causeway and then attack uphill. If he was defeated he would have the bog and the river behind him.

Baillie attacked the Royalist right, but was given little opportunity of regrouping after crossing the river, and at first the battle was furious with little advantage being gained by either side. Then Gordon's horse charged Balcarres on Baillie's left flank and was repulsed, the infantry supporting Balcarres drawing their swords and attacking the horses to hamstring them. Aboyne now attacked on the other flank with O'Kean's infantry, followed by the reserve, and Balcarres retreated rapidly. The Covenanter infantry, left unprotected on one flank and attacked on the other, were annihilated. Montrose had won another victory against superior odds, but his joy was tempered by the death of Lord Gordon in the fighting.

MAP 45

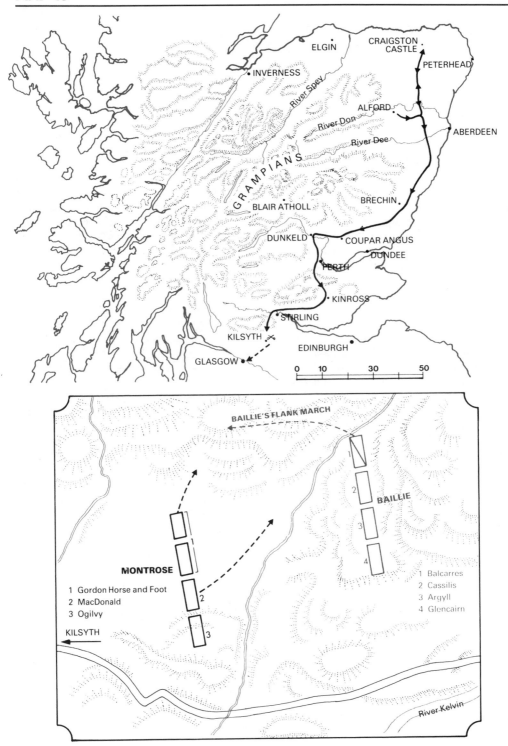

ELGIN
CRAIGSTON CASTLE
PETERHEAD
INVERNESS
River Spey
ALFORD
ABERDEEN
River Don
River Dee
G R A M P I A N S
BLAIR ATHOLL
BRECHIN
DUNKELD
COUPAR ANGUS
DUNDEE
PERTH
KINROSS
STIRLING
KILSYTH
EDINBURGH
GLASGOW

0   10   30   50

BAILLIE'S FLANK MARCH

BAILLIE

MONTROSE

1 Gordon Horse and Foot
2 MacDonald
3 Ogilvy

1 Balcarres
2 Cassilis
3 Argyll
4 Glencairn

KILSYTH

River Kelvin

MAP 45

The Battle of Kilsyth

8 July–15 August 1645

SIX days after the battle of Alford the Scottish parliament met in Stirling in considerable consternation because there was now only a small and largely raw Covenanter force under Lindsay in Scotland to oppose the victorious Montrose. Baillie offered his resignation but this was refused. Montrose had received news of the King's defeat at Naseby and saw the need to go to his assistance by marching into England. Meanwhile, he had received some new troops brought from the west by MacDonald and set off southwards to harry the parliament, which had now moved to Perth because of an outbreak of plague in Stirling. On 5 August Baillie seeing the coming disaster, again offered his resignation and this again was rejected. Aboyne rejoined Montrose at Dunkeld with a strong body of Gordon horse and foot, and Montrose, probably with his largest army yet, resolved to march southwards again, aiming by this move to draw the new Covenanter levies sufficiently far from home that they would probably desert. He advanced to Kinross, then turned westward, crossed the River Forth near Stirling and reached the outskirts of Kilsyth, only about 12 miles from Glasgow, on 14 August.

The Covenanters now had to fight. The Covenanting Committee, which accompanied the army, ignored Baillie's advice and marched across country instead of by the road, until Baillie, temporarily assuming command again, formed it up in a good position. He hoped that the Earl of Lanark, with a strong force, would reach him before the battle began, even though his army still outnumbered Montrose's by three to two.

On 15 August Montrose deployed in the valley below the hill on which the Covenanters stood, but this was not as dangerous as it may sound since the country was so rough that any attack downhill would inevitably be disorganised by the time that it reached him. The Covenanting Committee, consisting of Argyle, Elcho and Burleigh, who had all been the recipients of Montrose's wrath before, decided that it was better to entrap him to prevent him slipping away northwards than to launch a frontal assault against him.

The Covenanters now committed a blunder for which Montrose could never have hoped in his wildest dreams: they set out to march their army across Montrose's front and in his full view, to try to reach a hill behind him. A small body of Covenanters did attack down hill and was repulsed, and MacDonald charged uphill at the main army. Montrose, realising the Covenanters' intention, meanwhile had sent a body of foot on to the very hill which the Covenanters were trying to reach. The Highlanders attacked the flank of the advancing Covenanter army and destroyed it. The battle raged for a short while but soon the Lowlanders broke and fled, pursued by the Irishmen who gave them no quarter because some of their female camp followers had been butchered by the Covenanters a few days earlier.

Montrose had won another decisive victory and it seemed that at last he had fulfilled his boast of being master of all Scotland.

MAP 46

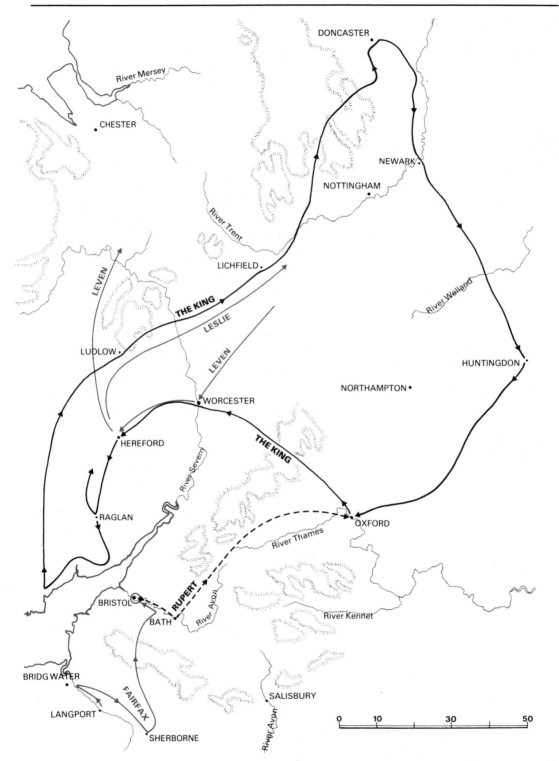

MAP 46

The Capture of Bristol

17 June–11 September 1645

FOLLOWING his victory at Langport, Fairfax laid siege to Bridgwater and then stormed the town after a heavy artillery bombardment. On 23 July he entered the town, thus severing all communications between the King and the Royalists in the southwest. He subsequently carried on to eliminate the remaining Royalist strongholds in Somerset except for Dunster castle.

The King had meanwhile moved to Raglan and there learned of the disasters in Somerset. With Leven nearing Worcester his position was becoming untenable and Charles resolved to march north again with the intention of joining Montrose in Scotland, although by this time Prince Rupert was urging him to sue for peace as the only way of preserving the kingdom. On 21 July Pontefract, and four days later Scarborough, had surrendered to the Roundheads, and in South Wales Haverford West, Milford Haven and the whole of Pembrokeshire was captured on 5 August after a crushing Royalist defeat. Only from Scotland was the news still good.

The King's northern march had taken him through Ludlow and Lichfield to Doncaster with Sir David Leslie in pursuit, and realising now the impracticability of the expedition he turned south again through Newark to Huntingdon. He could not stay there and returned to Oxford on 28 August.

Meanwhile Fairfax, having taken Bridgwater and sent a small force to capture Bath on 30 July, had made his way to Sherborne where he besieged the castle and captured it on 15 August. He now headed for Bristol and on 23 August opened the siege of the city, where Rupert was in charge of the defences. Leven, at Hereford, now also heard the news from Scotland and abandoned his siege; Charles moved into the town on 4 September, but was no nearer to raising the siege of Bristol as by now there were very few men prepared to be recruited to a defeated army.

Rupert was not prepared to surrender Bristol when called upon to do so, but his force was totally inadequate to defend it. On 10 September Fairfax began his assault on the city and captured the southern and eastern defences and the strong Priors Hill fort on the north. The Royalists set fire to part of the town but clearly could not hold out for very long, and Fairfax, not wanting to see unnecessary damage to the city or hardship to its inhabitants, offered fresh surrender terms which Rupert accepted; the city was handed over on 11 September. Rupert was allowed to march out with the honours of war and return to Oxford. Charles, not knowing the situation, was furious at what he considered as gross dereliction of duty, dismissed Rupert from all his commands and offices and exiled him.

In spite of the loss of Bristol the King was again considering marching to join up with Montrose. He did not intend to march into Scotland, but for Montrose, having subdued Scotland, to march into England, then with Goring's army they would make a last effort to reach London. On 18 September he set out once more from Raglan and on the following day Goring was ordered to march to Oxford. But it was one thing to give Goring orders and quite another to have them obeyed when Goring was enjoying himself in Exeter.

MAP 47

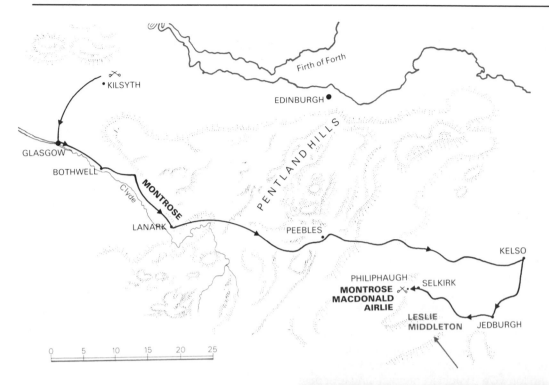

Sir David Leslie (1601-1682)

A Fifeshire man, he served in Sweden and returned to join
the Parliamentarians. He commanded the Scottish army in
England (finally defeating Montrose) and that which later
opposed Cromwell; he had a high military reputation. He
was imprisoned until the Restoration and then returned to
his estates. *In a private Scottish collection*

MAP 47

The Battle of Philiphaugh

July–18 September 1645

AFTER the battle of Kilsyth, Montrose, looking for more recruits, had rather foolishly marched his troops to Glasgow, but to his Highlanders the plunder in the city represented untold wealth and they soon ran amok. Nevertheless, by some strict punishments he regained control and marched them out again to Bothwell. This discontented the Highlanders, deprived of their booty, and within a few days the majority had deserted him again with such plunder as they had managed to collect. Aboyne, always faithful to Montrose, became furious when Montrose, apparently misunderstanding his man, appointed the Earl of Crawford as General of Horse, and Aboyne also left with most of the cavalry. Within a few weeks of the battle Montrose's army had been reduced, due to his own stupidity, to below its original strength and only numbered about 500 Irishmen and a few horse.

On 6 September David Leslie had crossed the border into Scotland with a large army, supported by Middleton. Montrose moved to Kelso in the hope of gaining recruits from the Border country, but still found it very difficult to recruit for his cause from the Covenanter-dominated Lowlands, and everything was very different from when the whole of Scotland appeared to be in his power. He marched to Jedburgh and then to Selkirk, all the while believing that Leslie was well to the north of him. But Leslie was not. He had turned quickly towards Montrose, whose patrols were ineffective and had not discovered the Covenanter army movements. Montrose camped at the village of Philiphaugh, and on 13 September Leslie attacked him there.

It was a foggy morning, and as Leslie's 4,000 horsemen charged out of the mist only the remainder of MacDonald's faithful Irishmen and a small body of horse under the Earl of Airlie stood fast. The remainder of his horse, over a thousand gentlemen who had recently joined him presumably for the possible benefits and certainly not to fight, made no effort to take part in the battle and left the field. Montrose's tiny army had little hope against Leslie's hordes. Although the Irishmen struggled for a while and fought bravely they were eventually overwhelmed, and Montrose, for the first time, had to leave the field in a hurry as the vanquished commander.

None of his army escaped. Those Irishmen alive after the battle were butchered by the victorious Covenanters along with their camp followers, wives and children. Leslie had taken a few prisoners, but the Covenanter leaders believed that clemency was weakness, and to their and Leslie's lasting shame he was forced to abandon these also to the butchery of the avenging Covenanter army and Committee.

Indefatigable as ever, Montrose tried to raise another army, but with no success. He carried on guerilla warfare with a few faithful throughout the winter and the spring of 1646, until on 31 May he received information that the King had surrendered himself to the Covenanters, and at the same time was ordered to lay down his arms. For a while he disobeyed, but at the end of July he met Middleton to arrange terms. His men were all to be pardoned, although Montrose himself, the Earl of Crawford and Sir John Hurry (who had changed sides once more) were to be exiled. They left the country on 3 September bound for Norway, the Covenanter leaders in Edinburgh trying to ignore the surrender terms and prevent them from getting away.

MAP 48

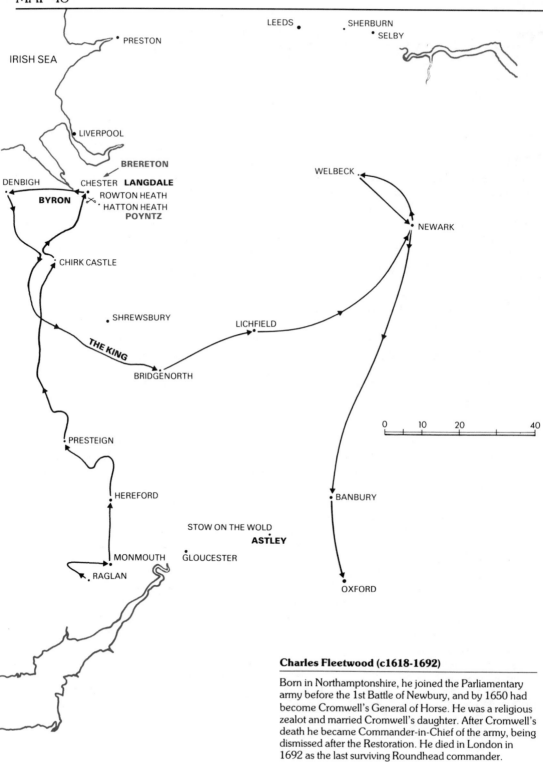

LEEDS
SHERBURN
SELBY

PRESTON

IRISH SEA

LIVERPOOL

BRERETON

DENBIGH
CHESTER **LANGDALE**
BYRON
ROWTON HEATH
HATTON HEATH
POYNTZ

WELBECK

NEWARK

CHIRK CASTLE

SHREWSBURY
LICHFIELD

THE KING

BRIDGENORTH

0   10   20   40

PRESTEIGN

HEREFORD

STOW ON THE WOLD
ASTLEY

BANBURY

MONMOUTH
GLOUCESTER

RAGLAN

OXFORD

Charles Fleetwood (c1618-1692)

Born in Northamptonshire, he joined the Parliamentary
army before the 1st Battle of Newbury, and by 1650 had
become Cromwell's General of Horse. He was a religious
zealot and married Cromwell's daughter. After Cromwell's
death he became Commander-in-Chief of the army, being
dismissed after the Restoration. He died in London in
1692 as the last surviving Roundhead commander.

MAP 48

The Campaign of Rowton Heath

18 September–5 November 1645

CHARLES marched through the Welsh hills with his weary army to Presteign, and on 22 September he reached Chirk castle. Here he learned that a Roundhead attack on Chester had been repulsed and marched there at once, entering the city the following night. Langdale, with his horse, was sent to take up a position two miles to the southeast on Rowton Heath. The Roundheads, under General Sydenham Poyntz, were however, pursuing the King and arrived at Hatton Heath a couple of miles from Rowton on the morning of 24 September. Both forces were composed entirely of cavalry. The country between them was very bad for cavalry, with small fields and high hedges, but as the Royalists did not appear to intend to leave their position Poyntz advanced to attack them.

The battle was fierce and at first Langdale was driven back, but he rallied his men and eventually Poyntz in his turn was forced to withdraw. At this point he was joined by a small body of musketeers from the force which had attacked Chester, and now, with infantry to support him, he had an advantage over his adversary. Poyntz charged again and another desperate struggle ensued. Then a volley of musketry scattered Langdale's horse and they fled with Poyntz in pursuit. Lord Lichfield brought a party from the city to Langdale's aid but in the end this body too was driven back and Lichfield was killed. The Royalists had suffered another significant defeat.

Chester was still defended by Lord Byron, although its days must now be numbered, and Charles rode to Denbigh with his remaining 2,500 horse to await events. Although he could not now see how to continue his march towards Scotland, he could not sit still for long, and his next plan was to cross the country to Newark and there await Montrose. But this was a vain hope because of the changed situation in Scotland, of which he did not know when he started out, the tidings of the battle of Philiphaugh not reaching him until he was on the way to Newark.

After the capture of Bristol, Cromwell had been sent to seize the various remaining Royalist strongholds in Hampshire and Wiltshire. Devizes castle had been taken on 23 September, Berkeley castle surrendered three days later, and on the 28th he entered Winchester (see Map 43). On 11 October he was at Basing House, which had been held for the King throughout the war, and having summoned it to surrender without success, bombarded it with his siege guns. On 14 October he stormed the mansion through the breaches made by the guns, the house was sacked and burnt and many of the defenders were killed. The rest were taken prisoner, among whom were the great architect Inigo Jones and the owner of the house, the Catholic Marquess of Winchester. Cromwell then turned westwards and rejoined Fairfax at Crediton on 24 October.

Sir Edward Massey (1619-1675)

Born in Cheshire, he joined the King in 1642 but soon changed sides: he was a zealous Presbyterian and opposed the King on religious grounds. An energetic Roundhead leader he nevertheless believed in conciliation. After the war he fell out with Parliament, was impeached but escaped abroad. He joined Charles II in his abortive invasion, was captured and again escaped, returning at the Restoration.

MAP 49

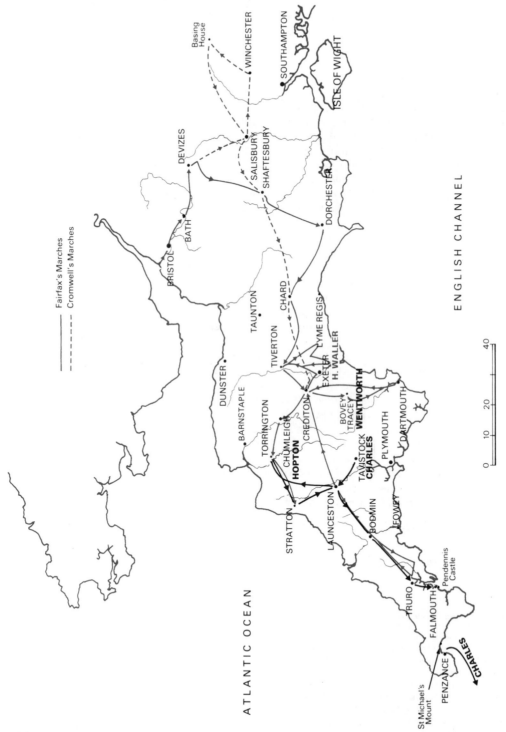

MAP 49

The Final Campaign in the Southwest

October 1645–20 April 1646

I N THE west Goring's health had at last succumbed to his high living and in November he left for France. The Prince of Wales took command of his army and assembled it round Tavistock; it was a strong force numerically, with 5,000 horse and 6,000 foot, but was raw and largely untrained. Meanwhile Fairfax had set off for the west at the beginning of October, leaving a cavalry force to watch Oxford. He too had his problems because of the shortage of money, without which his troops refused to go on, and spent a week at Chard until the treasure convoy arrived.

Normally, winter campaigning over muddy roads was almost impossible, but it was a hard winter and the mud was frozen, which made movement easier, and Fairfax began the last campaign in the southwest in January 1646. He advanced into Devon and Cornwall surprising part of Lord Wentworth's cavalry brigade near Bovey Tracy; it was scattered, Wentworth went back to Tavistock with his news and the Prince of Wales fell back to Launceston. Hopton was now made Commander-in-Chief of the western Cavalier army — a task which he realised could only end in his defeat — with Wentworth in command of the horse and Grenville of the infantry. But Grenville refused to serve under Hopton and the Prince, tired of his attitude, dismissed him for disobedience and imprisoned him in St Michael's Mount at Penzance.

Fairfax turned south and on 18 February in heavy snow stormed Dartmouth castle. From there he returned to besiege Exeter and at last was able to gain some recruits for the Roundheads in the west, promising clemency to the local populace who had suffered for too long under Goring and Grenville to support the Royalists as strongly as they had done in the past. Hopton moved north to Torrington, hoping to join up with the Royalists garrison of Barnstaple, but Fairfax got news of this manoeuvre and, leaving a small body under Sir Hardress Waller to carry on with the siege of Exeter, but with still over 10,000 men, marched after him.

On 21 February Fairfax reached Chumleigh and two days later, in pouring rain, began skirmishing with the Royalist outposts. Without further delay he attacked Torrington that night and the Royalist horse broke, Hopton being unable to stem the flight. The King's cause in the west was sealed when the powder magazine stored in the church blew up, leaving Hopton with no ammunition and little hope of getting any more. It was the death knell of the western Royalist army.

Hopton, in defeat, retreated to Stratton, the scene of his first victory. Fairfax entered Launceston on 25 February and Hopton's army was now melting away rapidly. On 1 March Hopton abandoned Bodmin whence he had again fallen back, Fairfax entering the town on his heels, and retired to Pendennis castle at Falmouth and St Michael's Mount. The Prince of Wales sailed for the Scilly Isles, where he would be safe from Fairfax, and now Hopton's task was finished. On 6 March Fairfax offered terms of surrender, on 10 March he entered Truro and on 20 March Hopton surrendered and his army was disbanded. Fairfax returned to Exeter and on 13 April the city, the capital of the west, surrendered, followed by St Michael's Mount two days later, and Barnstaple and Dunster castle on 20 April.

MAP 50

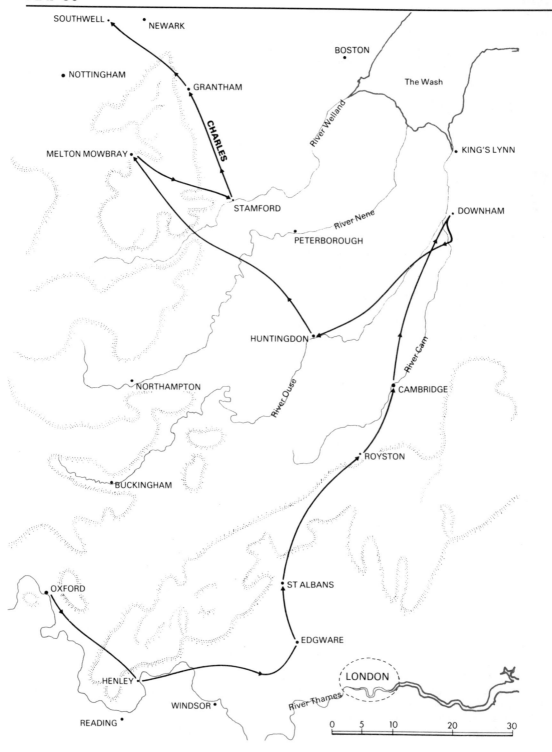

SOUTHWELL

NEWARK

NOTTINGHAM

GRANTHAM

CHARLES

BOSTON

The Wash

River Welland

KING'S LYNN

MELTON MOWBRAY

STAMFORD

River Nene

DOWNHAM

PETERBOROUGH

HUNTINGDON

River Ouse

River Cam

NORTHAMPTON

CAMBRIDGE

ROYSTON

BUCKINGHAM

ST ALBANS

OXFORD

EDGWARE

HENLEY

LONDON

WINDSOR

River Thames

READING

0   5   10   20   30

MAP 50

The Last Days of the First Civil War

1 October 1645–3 September 1646

AT BRIDGNORTH on 1 October Charles heard of Montrose's disaster at Philiphaugh, but he did not believe it. Three days later the King was at the Royalist stronghold of Newark. After resting there he marched north as far as Welbeck Abbey where he received Montrose's dispatch confirming his defeat. To go farther north was obviously impractical, with no Royalist Scottish army left and with Leslie, Leven and the Roundhead Scottish army in the Borders and Northumberland. He did however order Langdale's Yorkshire horse to join Montrose in the hope of salvaging some of his cause in Scotland.

Charles returned to Newark on 15 October. Poyntz had been following — as Charles had hoped he would, to take the pressure off Chester — but did not realise that he was so close to the King. On 15 October a body of Poyntz's foot was surprised, attacked and routed at Sherburn, between Selby and Leeds (see Map 48), although the Royalist success was short-lived because Langdale's horse, which had not yet left for Scotland, panicked and fled when they had almost gained the victory, through a misunderstanding with Digby. Digby (ever the over-optimist in his councils to the King) and his horse also fled and made for Scotland. The King left Newark on 3 November and marched back to Oxford which he entered on the 5th.

The war was rapidly coming to an end with total defeat for the Royalists. In the northwest Chester at last surrendered to Brereton on 3 February 1646, and on 21 March the Roundhead force released from its siege surprised Lord Astley — who was making for Oxford from Worcester — at Stow-on-the-Wold and soon overwhelmed him, Astley himself being taken prisoner.

In March 1646 the King entered into secret negotiations with the Convenanters in which he offered to surrender to them if they would grant him safety. The negotiations were protracted and it was not until 27 April that Charles, disguised as a servant, left Oxford. His route meandered first towards London and then northwards through St Albans, heading for King's Lynn. Perhaps he hoped to escape from there by sea, but in fact got no farther than Downham. Presumably abandoning the idea, he made his way by a devious route via Melton Mowbray and Stamford to Southwell, whence the Scots had sent an escort to meet him. On 5 May the King was a prisoner.

On 6 May Newark surrendered, having been invested by Leven and Poyntz after the King's departure the previous November, and Sir David Leslie, freed from his responsibilities there, undertook fresh ones by taking over the Royal captive and setting off to Newcastle. Parliament, having known nothing of Charles's dealings with the Scots but being suspicious, demanded that he be handed over to them, but for some time this was refused.

On 24 June Prince Rupert, who had returned to join the King at the beginning of the year, handed over Oxford to the Roundheads. The last Royalist strongholds in England to surrender were Pendennis castle and Raglan, both of which were bravely defended to the last. Pendennis capitulated on 16 August, after being virtually starved out, and Raglan was captured on 19 August. On 16 September 1646 the Earl of Essex died, having just lived until the end of the war.

The Situation after the First Civil War

December 1646–February 1648

BY DECEMBER 1646 the Scots had accepted that the King would not take the Covenant and agreed that he should be handed over to Parliament. But Parliament did not want him in London where he might raise a following, and decided that he should be lodged at Holmby House near Althorp in Northamptonshire. He left Newcastle on 3 February 1647 and travelled by easy stages escorted by the Parliamentary Commissioners. The King had gained favour in the north during the Scottish occupation and people rejoiced as he passed and bells were rung. At Nottingham Fairfax met him and kissed hands and even the gentry of Puritan Northamptonshire greeted him enthusiastically.

At the end of the war Parliament had decided to retain the New Model Army for only six months, although some Welsh castles had not yet been captured. Denbigh did not capitulate until 26 October 1646, Chirk until 28 February 1647, and Harlech, the last of Charles's fortifications still to fly his Standard, held out until 13 March 1647. In February 1647 this matter came under discussion, and it was decided that the cavalry only should be retained and that for infantry Parliament would have to rely on the Trained Bands.

Fortified towns would be opened, with the exception of a few major fortresses, and this would reduce the number of troops required for garrison duties. Of the regiments being disbanded many volunteered to join an army being formed to go to Ireland. In March 1647 there were troubles in the Parliamentary army, partly because of arrears of pay through a shortage of money and partly because of a power struggle between the Presbyterian commanders and the strict Puritan ones, the Independents, under the control of Cromwell.

Parliament believed in June that a Scottish plot was being hatched to carry off the King from Holmby either back to Scotland or to London, and a certain Cornet Joyce, almost certainly on Cromwell's orders, was sent to Holmby ostensibly to guard against any such scheme. Joyce surrounded and entered the house and later asked Charles to accompany him to another place, his only authority being the cavalry escort he had brought with him. He abducted the King and took him to Newmarket, near where Fairfax was holding a general assembly of the army.

Parliament, only hearing of this when Charles was on his way, intuitively guessed that Cromwell was the perpetrator of the plot and there was talk of impeaching him; but Cromwell slipped away and also made for Newmarket. Fairfax was ordered to return the King to Holmby and sent a force to intercept him and to protect him from insult. Charles frustrated this intention by going to Childerly, near Cambridge, and refusing to return to Holmby, even though Fairfax rode over and tried to persuade him. He demanded to go to his own house at Newmarket, to which Fairfax agreed.

Also in June, feeling in the army against its lack of pay was growing and it decided to take matters into its own hands and marched to Royston, its spokesmen proclaiming that it did not want to alter the system of government but merely to get paid. Parliament attempted to raise money to stop the mutineers — Fairfax's veterans — from reaching London. The army marched on southwards and although the Trained Bands were called out very few appeared to answer the summons, and the City was extremely perturbed. Parliament sent the army a month's pay and the crisis died down for the time being.

The Scottish parliament now offered the

King to send an army into England to help him, but he refused the aid because he guessed, rightly, that the conditions would be for him to embrace Presbyterianism. The King had meanwhile been moved to Caversham, at Reading, and Parliament was attempting to come to terms with him through Sir John Berkeley as mediator. On 19 July Fairfax was reconfirmed as Commander-in-Chief and his army was purged of its agitators.

Parliament, still controlled by the Presbyterians, had agreed that the City should control its own militia, but this did not suit the army or some of the outer boroughs of London, and the army under Fairfax entered the city on 6 August and took over control to prevent disturbances. By August the Independents had won their struggle and many of the older commanders, men such as Waller, Stapleton and Massey, were having to flee the country. The people, even those in London, were tired of the harsh rule of Parliament and asked for the return of the King.

From Hatfield the King had been moved to Hampton Court, still under guard by the army, and while Parliament was debating the political situation during August he escaped and fled to the Isle of Wight. Presumably he felt that he would be in a better position to negotiate if he were free, and anyway might be able to find a ship to allow him to escape to France. There were still plenty of Royalist supporters — or if not strictly Royalist at least anti-Puritan — and these were encouraged surreptitiously to rearm and to be ready for action.

In February 1648 there were risings in support of the King in various parts of the country. There was active revolt in South Wales, and the Roundhead governor of Pembroke castle, Colonel Poyer, declared himself for the King and seized most of Pembrokeshire. In Scotland the King was becoming more popular and a new army was being raised. Sir Marmaduke Langdale surprised and captured Berwick with a small party and advanced into Lancashire, whilst another party took Carlisle. There had also been outbreaks of Royalist fervour in Kent, where it was now apparent that the King would have got support during the war if his armies had only been able to get there, and in Essex and in the west country. Most of the local forces of Parliament had by now been disbanded and only the New Model Army, much truncated, remained. A dangerous situation was facing Parliament, and what became known as the Second Civil War began.

MAP 51

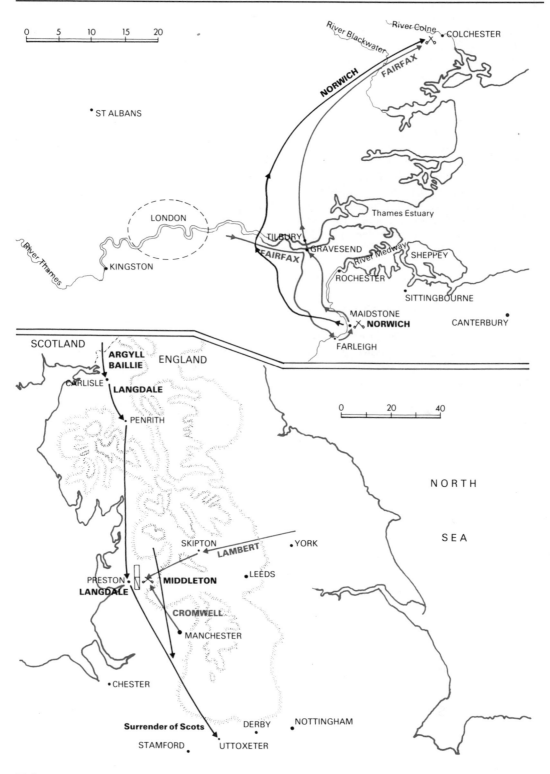

0 5 10 15 20

River Blackwater

River Colne

• COLCHESTER

NORWICH

FAIRFAX

• ST ALBANS

Thames Estuary

LONDON

TILBURY

FAIRFAX

GRAVESEND

River Thames

River Medway

SHEPPEY

KINGSTON

ROCHESTER

SITTINGBOURNE

CANTERBURY •

MAIDSTONE

NORWICH

FARLEIGH

SCOTLAND

ARGYLL BAILLIE

ENGLAND

CARLISLE •

LANGDALE

• PENRITH

0 20 40

N O R T H

S E A

SKIPTON

LAMBERT

• YORK

• LEEDS

PRESTON •

MIDDLETON

LANGDALE

CROMWELL

• MANCHESTER

• CHESTER

Surrender of Scots

DERBY •

NOTTINGHAM •

STAMFORD •

UTTOXETER

MAP 51

The Second Civil War

May–September 1648

FAIRFAX sent Cromwell into South Wales to crush the revolt, and the garrison of Newcastle was reinforced as a buffer against the Scots and Langdale. The Scottish parliament demanded that the New Model Army should be purged of all the Independents and asked for negotiations to be opened with the King, but of course these demands were refused. In May 1648 the rebellion in South Wales was put down, and Cromwell had taken Pembroke and Chepstow castles by 11 July.

Now the revolt blazed up in Kent and the Royalists seized a number of towns. Fairfax immediately set out to put down the revolt. He advanced to Gravesend and then turned south. The Earl of Norwich, Goring's father but no soldier, massed his 11,000 troops (of which 7,000 were not much better than an armed mob and were kept in reserve) around Maidstone. On 1 June Fairfax bypassed the town, crossed the River Medway at Farleigh bridge to the southwest and then turned back northwards to attack the town. The fight raged furiously all evening and Maidstone was defended desperately. By midnight all was over for Norwich, and the reserve, which took no part in the battle, had melted away.

The remainder of Norwich's troops retreated towards London and crossed the river into Essex where there had been a new rising, and marched to Colchester. Fairfax rode after them and attacked near the town on 13 July, where the Royalists had taken up a position athwart the London road, but initially made little progress against the resolute Cavalier foot. Despite this, the Royalists had had heavy casualties and now withdrew into the town, which after a siege was stormed and surrendered on 26 August.

On 8 July the Scottish army, 40,000 men strong but commanded by Argyll and other incompetents (except for Baillie who was now in a subordinate position), crossed the Border and was joined at Carlisle by Langdale. It advanced slowly and Cromwell was sent to the north. The Roundhead army under John Lambert marched through Skipton and the Royalist army continued southwards in Lancashire, very dispersed since many of the men were foraging, and on 16 August both armies were near Preston in pouring rain.

Despairing of Argyll taking any overt action, Langdale drew up his small force near the town, and Cromwell took up a position to oppose him. He attacked Langdale and in desperate fighting the Roundheads suffered severe casualties. Nevertheless, at length strength of numbers told, Argyll having done nothing to come to the Royalists' aid, and Langdale's valiant troops began to give way; the retreat soon turned into a rout. Cromwell entered Preston and set off south in pursuit of the Scots, whom Middleton and his horse had joined but could do nothing to stem their retreat. The Scottish army, not having fought at all, was forced to surrender at Uttoxeter.

The Prince of Wales now sailed for the Downs with the Royalist fleet and met Warwick, once more Lord High Admiral, in the mouth of the Thames. The Prince wanted to bring him to action and win a decisive victory which might have brought the people of London out on his side, but the wind changed and he was forced to sail away to Holland.

The Second Civil War was over and Cromwell crossed the Border and occupied Edinburgh. Had the Royalist risings been better co-ordinated and better commanded they might have had success, but Fairfax's control of the Roundhead army was so superior that the result was a foregone conclusion in spite of moments of worry and panic by Parliament.

MAP 52

WICK

Loch
Assynt
ARDVRECK CASTLE

Loch Shin

MONTROSE'S ESCAPE

LAIRG

MONTROSE

DUNROBIN CASTLE

Kyle of
Sutherland

SUTHERLAND

Dornoch Firth

STRACHAN

TAIN

LESLIE

Cromarty Firth

Moray Firth

ELGIN

NAIRN

Beauly Firth

INVERNESS

Loch Ness

0   5   10   15   25

The Third Civil War

MAP 52

Montrose's Last Battle

23 March–21 May 1650

CHARLES I was executed on 31 January 1649, and five days later Charles II was, dejure, proclaimed King in Scotland. However, he was not allowed to exercise his position until he had embraced the Covenant and given an undertaking that he would encourage Presbyterianism. This he was not yet prepared to do and decided on one last attempt to avoid it. He appointed Montrose as his Commander-in-Chief in Scotland, although this was obviously not endorsed by the Scots.

With great difficulty Montrose was trying to raise an army with which to return to Scotland, and with some Danish and German mercenaries he landed in Orkney on 23 March 1650, where he gained a few Orcadian recruits. Montrose, with Hurry serving under him and acting as advance guard commander, crossed to the mainland and began a march southwards through Sutherland towards Inverness.

When David Leslie, now commanding the Scottish army for the Covenanters, heard of the landing he concentrated his army near Brechin and then marched north, being joined by some Monroes and Rosses (who Montrose believed were going to support him) and at Tain by the Earl of Sutherland. The latter was sent north of the Dornoch Firth to the Kyle of Sutherland, an inlet on the western end of the Firth, to harrass Montrose's communications; while Strachan, the commander at Inverness, marched up the south side to attack the Royalists.

Montrose had marched down the coast from Wick, had unsuccessfully summoned Dunrobin castle, the home of the Sutherlands, to surrender, and on 27 April was at the head of the Kyle of Sutherland. He took up a position there on the slopes of a hill with Strachan two or three miles away to the south. Montrose had had no Highland recruits and was very weak; Strachan knew this and concealed most of his army, only allowing one troop of horse to be seen. Montrose assumed, from his meagre intelligence sources, that this was all the army he had to face and moved his small force forward on to the flat ground. As soon as Montrose was off his hill Strachan attacked him with his hidden horsemen.

The Orcadians fled without offering any resistance, and the mercenaries fell back to the hillside, where the Monroes and Rosses, waiting to make sure that they were on the winning side, attacked and routed them. In spite of Montrose's horse fighting bravely they too were soon overwhelmed and Hurry was captured. Montrose, wounded, escaped, and crossing the mountains reached Ardvreck castle on Loch Assynt. There he was betrayed and handed over to the Covenanters by the Laird, Neil Macleod, on 30 April.

Montrose was taken to Edinburgh where on 21 May he was executed. On 23 June Charles II landed in Moray and accepted the Covenant, thus betraying all that Montrose had attempted to do for him and for his father before him. He marched to Edinburgh and on 15 July was, defacto, proclaimed King.

MAP 53

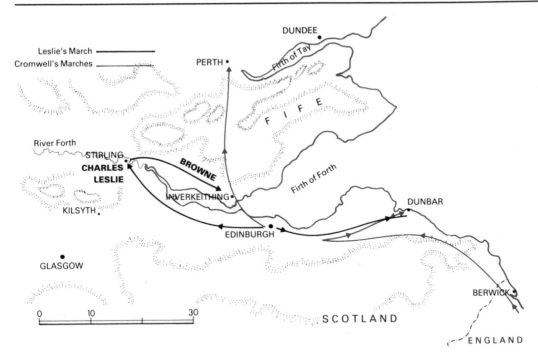

Sir Henry Ireton (1611-1651)

Born near Nottingham, he joined the Parliamentarians in 1642 and was a close adherent of Cromwell, whose eldest daughter he married in 1646. He approved of the monarchy but not the King, and was a regicide. He became Cromwell's deputy in Ireland but overwork caused his early death.

Sir James Lumsden (1598-1660)

A Scot, like many of his time he served with the Swedish army. He joined the Roundheads, was a competent commander, and wrote a contemporary account of Marston Moor, where he contributed greatly to the victory. He later joined David Leslie and was captured at Dunbar, although later released.

MAP 53

The Approach to Dunbar

28 June–18 August 1650

FOR some time it had been apparent to Parliament that it would have to send an army to subdue the Scots; this became a necessity once Charles II landed there and was proclaimed King. Although Fairfax was still the Commander-in-Chief of the Roundhead army he was unwilling to participate in a long and gruelling campaign, and so Cromwell, who had recently returned from laying waste the Irish Catholics, was appointed as Commander of the army with John Lambert as second in command and Monck as General of Foot. A number of new Parliamentary regiments were raised so that England would not be left undefended against any further Royalist rising.

Cromwell set off from London on 28 June, concentrating near Berwick and then crossing the Border three weeks later with a well-commanded and well-trained army of 16,000 men, subsequently reduced by sickness to about 12,000, which advanced to the outskirts of Edinburgh. As soon as news reached the Scots of Cromwell's march they began recruiting rapidly and eventually built up a force of over 20,000 men: but it was a raw and untrained army, and, apart from Leslie himself, its commander, the officers were poor, having been appointed more on religious that military grounds after the debacle at Preston two years earlier. The Scottish army was also mostly composed of Lowlanders who by and large were not such tough fighters as the Highlanders.

Being repulsed, Cromwell withdrew from Edinburgh and Leslie followed him up with an attack by his horse. Charges and counter-charges followed and the result was indecisive, although Cromwell could get no nearer to the city. The summer in Scotland was very wet and cold, and the Parliamentary army was suffering from the weather as well as a shortage of supplies. Leslie was prepared to wait during August and by the end of the month Cromwell was in a serious state. He had retired on the small port of Dunbar, and while it would have been a loss of prestige to have had to retreat over the Border again, to stay during the winter would have been to court disaster.

The heavy rain continued. On 18 August Cromwell marched back to Edinburgh, but Leslie had taken up a strong position near Corstorphine and in spite of several attacks Cromwell achieved nothing; he had been out-manoeuvred and out-generalled by Leslie. Seeing Cromwell's weakened state Leslie now decided to advance against him.

On 2 September Leslie followed along the coast and took up a strong position on Doon Hill, south of Dunbar and blocking Cromwell's road back to England. If Leslie had stayed where he was, Cromwell would either have had to retreat or embark his army on the ships waiting in the harbour, but Leslie, encouraged by the Covenanting Committee, wanted the glory of a decisive victory. To obtain this he had to move down on to the flat ground, where Cromwell's army was drawn up, and attack him. Leslie had made a terrible and fatal mistake.

MAP 54

DUNBAR

LESLIE

Brox Burn

Doon Hill

1 Cromwell
2 Monck
2 Lambert
4 Fleetwood

0   ½   1   1½   2

MAP 54 *(See also Map 53)*

The Battle of Dunbar and its Aftermath

3 September 1650–2 August 1651

BEFORE Leslie could get properly organised at Dunbar, Cromwell decided to attack at dawn on 3 September. His plan was for a frontal assault by Monck's foot supported by Lambert and Fleetwood, and a flanking movement on the right, where Leslie was restricted by the Brox Burn and the hill, by a mixed body of horse and foot. Cromwell with another mixed force was to move on to Leslie's right flank. It was still pouring with rain, and the attack was to be carried out with the utmost stealth.

The battle opened with a heavy charge by the Roundhead cavalry under Lambert and Fleetwood, but it was driven back. At first the Roundhead foot too were driven off, and very little advantage was being gained on the flank. The Scots fought with fierce determination, but then came another cavalry charge on the Scots' left which sent the Scottish horse scattering among the infantry, creating confusion. The Scots were now cramped for space and a furious battle raged for nearly two hours. By then, after heavy casualties, the Scottish army had been crushed and Cromwell had won what was probably his greatest victory, although it was largely given to him by Leslie's blunder. For very small losses to his own army he had killed around 3,000 Scots and taken another 10,000 prisoner.

Charles, who was at Stirling, was not dismayed by the Scots' defeat because this was a Covenanter army; he saw that they would have to turn to him and a Royalist army being recruited in the Highlands if the Roundheads were to be driven out of Scotland. He was again being optimistic.

Cromwell advanced on Edinburgh again and occupied the city, but Edinburgh castle still held out against him.

During the winter the Scots built up a strong position at Stirling and Cromwell marched to and fro between Edinburgh and Glasgow, being able to do nothing to bring the Scots to battle. At Christmas 1650 Edinburgh castle at last capitulated, although that did not help Cromwell very much, and in February 1651 he became seriously ill and did not recover until the summer.

During the spring and summer of 1651 Leslie, with his newly built-up army, tempted the Roundheads to attack him, but was always able to fall back to Stirling in time to avoid battle having learned his lesson at Dunbar; only the occasional skirmish resulted. Cromwell now saw that his one hope was to outflank Stirling and to cut Leslie off from his supplies in Fife and the north, which might induce Leslie to leave his prepared position, and on 17 July a small force was sent across the Forth.

Leslie dispatched Sir John Browne with 4,000 troops to drive the Roundheads back, but in a sharp and fiercely contested battle at Inverkeithing Browne was routed by Lambert. Leslie now fell into the trap prepared for him and moved his whole army against Lambert, but again quickly saw his error and retreated to Stirling, leaving the way open for Cromwell to march north and capture Perth on 2 August. Here Cromwell learned that Leslie had outmanoeuvred him again, and the Scottish army, no longer being watched, marched out of Stirling and was on its way to England.

MAP 55

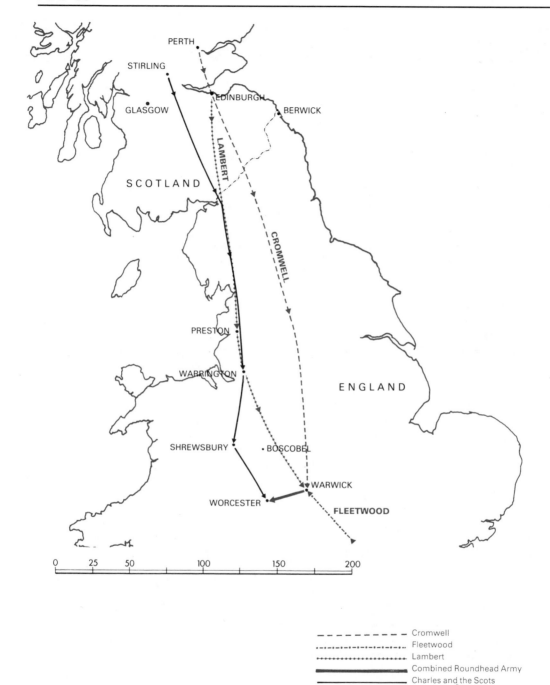

PERTH

STIRLING

GLASGOW

EDINBURGH

BERWICK

LAMBERT

SCOTLAND

CROMWELL

PRESTON

WARRINGTON

ENGLAND

SHREWSBURY

BOSCOBEL

WARWICK

WORCESTER

FLEETWOOD

| 0 | 25 | 50 | 100 | 150 | 200 |

------ Cromwell
-----·----- Fleetwood
········· Lambert
━━━━━━ Combined Roundhead Army
──────── Charles and the Scots

MAP 55

The Roads to Worcester

6 August–3 September 1651

WHEN Leslie left Stirling and crossed into England on 6 August 1651 it was not of his own volition. He did not believe that leaving Scotland with Cromwell still in possession of Perth and Edinburgh was sensible, and would have preferred to give battle with superior numbers on ground of his own choosing between Perth and Edinburgh. In this belief he was supported by the Duke of Hamilton and other leading Scotsmen, but the King was determined to carry the fight into England with the presumed intention of eventually reaching London. His army was about 16,000 strong.

Early action by Parliament was imperative in case the Royalists in England flocked to the new King, and therefore Cromwell marched south from Perth, not pursuing the Royalists too closely while he made his plans, and crossed the Forth on 4 August. Lambert was ordered to catch up with and harrass the Scots as soon as possible and Monck was left in Scotland to hold Edinburgh and to capture Stirling; at the same time Fleetwood was collecting another army around London, and Harrison was in Lancashire. Lambert and Harrison joined forces near Preston and fell back before the Royalists to Warrington, while Cromwell advanced across the Tyne on 13 August and carried on south, meeting up with Lambert at Warwick on 24 August. Cromwell was determined to collect as large as possible before giving battle and to defeat Charles once and for all.

Charles also carried on southwards, unsuccessfully summoning Shrewsbury to surrender and bypassing the town, and entered Worcester on 23 August. He had gained virtually no recruits since the Covenanting Committee had issued a statement that no man could be enlisted who did not take the Covenant, and there was very little support for this among the Royalists. At Worcester he decided to rest, gather what reinforcements he could from Wales and to resupply his army. He also decided to fortify the city, throwing up earthworks and depending on the River Severn as a defence line. Cromwell slowly drew a net around Worcester and when Fleetwood joined him his army numbered about 28,000 men, twice the size of the Royalist one. Cromwell now planned for Fleetwood and Lambert to cross the Severn south of the city and to advance northwards, while he and the rest of the army formed up on the east bank and on Red Hill facing west.

The Royalists were already in some disarray, as Buckingham was sulking and Leslie, who did not want to be there, hung back and complained of the lack of fighting quality of his troops when they were outside Scotland. Charles, now in command of the whole army decided to attack the battery on Red Hill which had started to bombard the city. The attack was not a success as the plan had been 'leaked', and he was repulsed. Lambert now crossed the river well south of the city at Upton, where he was opposed, but he quickly beat off the enemy and advanced northwards, being followed across by Fleetwood and by a mixed force under Deane.

MAP 56

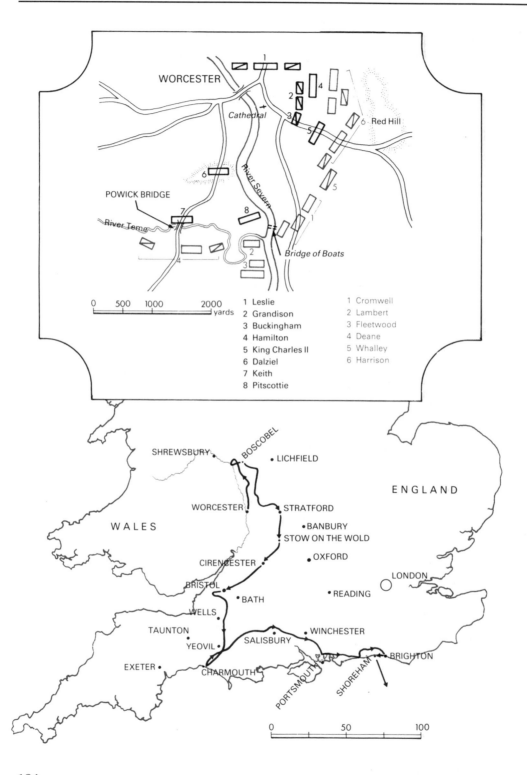

WORCESTER

Cathedral

6· Red Hill

River Severn

POWICK BRIDGE

River Teme

Bridge of Boats

0	500	1000	2000

yards

1 Leslie
2 Grandison
3 Buckingham
4 Hamilton
5 King Charles II
6 Dalziel
7 Keith
8 Pitscottie

1 Cromwell
2 Lambert
3 Fleetwood
4 Deane
5 Whalley
6 Harrison

SHREWSBURY
BOSCOBEL
• LICHFIELD

ENGLAND

WORCESTER
• STRATFORD

WALES

• BANBURY
STOW ON THE WOLD

CIRENCESTER

• OXFORD

BRISTOL

LONDON

• BATH
• READING

WELLS

TAUNTON
YEOVIL
SALISBURY
• WINCHESTER

EXETER •

CHARMOUTH

PORTSMOUTH

SHOREHAM

BRIGHTON

0	50	100

MAP 56

The Battle of Worcester and the Escape of Charles II

3 September–15 October 1651

I T WAS 3 September, the anniversary of Dunbar and subsequently to be the date of Cromwell's death, but it was also a coincidence that the first and last battles of the Civil Wars were to be fought near Powick Bridge (see Map 2), as of course happened over 200 years later around Mons. The plan on the west bank of the river was for Deane to take Powick Bridge over the River Teme and for Lambert to cross the river on a bridge of boats nearby. For the Royalists Keith held the bridge whilst Pitscottie and his Highlanders opposed the bridge of boats. Dalziel's brigade was in reserve on higher ground.

The fighting on the River Teme was furious and desperate and the Roundheads were repeatedly thrown back, but a second bridge of boats had been built across the Severn just above its junction with the Teme and over this Cromwell now led his infantry. The High-landers fought gallantly and with great determination but were gradually forced to retire by the combination of Lambert and Cromwell; Keith, with his left flank now unprotected, was also forced to withdraw. Dalziel did not manage to stem the retreat and soon it became a rout with the Royalists streaming back towards the city.

Now that the Roundhead position on the east bank had been weakened by Cromwell's river crossing, Charles seized the opportunity to attack the Roundhead right wing with Hamilton's brigade, Buckingham and Grandi-son supporting him with cavalry. It was in fact a brilliant attack and the battle raged for three hours, the Parliamentary army giving ground all the while, and it might have succeeded if Leslie had brought his brigade and his cavalry into action. Eventually Cromwell recrossed the river and came to the assistance of his right flank: this turned the tide, the Royalists being driven back to the city in confusion.

Charles tried to rally his regiments and there was fighting in the streets of the city, but by now the Roundheads were pressing on all sides and the battle was to all intents over. The Royalist army attempted to escape northwards through the only gate still in its possession, but it was overwhelmed, with heavy casualties (particularly to the Scots). Around 10,000 prisoners were taken, and most of the Royalist commanders were also captured, in some cases remaining in captivity for many years.

Charles himself managed to escape through a fierce rearguard action by a small body of Cavaliers under the Earl of Cleveland, hero of Cropredy Bridge. The legends are many of Charles II's subsequently hiding in the oak tree at Boscobel, near Shifnal in Shropshire, until he could make his way across the country and overseas again. After attempting unsuccess-fully to escape via Lyme Regis, he eventually sailed with Lord Wilmot, who had accom-panied him on all his travels, from Shoreham to France on 15 October, after six weeks of adventurous wandering and excitements. Charles did not appear in England again until his restoration nine years later.

Index